Americans and Climate Change

Closing the Gap Between
Science and Action

A Synthesis of Insights and Recommendations
from the 2005 Yale F&ES Conference on Climate Change

Daniel R. Abbasi
With a Foreword by James Gustave Speth

**YALE SCHOOL OF FORESTRY & ENVIRONMENTAL STUDIES
PUBLICATION SERIES**

Title	*Americans and Climate Change: Closing the Gap between Science and Action*
Volume author	Daniel R. Abbasi
Book design	Peter W. Johnson and Maura Gianakos, YaleRIS
Cover design	Maura Gianakos, YaleRIS
Cover image	The image on the cover is a snapshot from a climate simulation model that runs from 1920-2080. The model is being run by harnessing desktop computers around the world at climateprediction.net, a collaborative project of the University of Oxford, the Hadley Centre for Climate Prediction and others. Used with permission. To participate in the model using your desktop computer, go to: *www.climateprediction.net*
Page layout	Dorothy Scott, North Branford, CT
Print on demand	Yale Reprographics and Imaging Services (RIS)
Publication series editor	Jane Coppock
Paper	Mohawk Creme 30% recycled ♻
To obtain copies	This book is available as a free downloadable pdf at *www.yale.edu/environment/publications*. Hard copies may be ordered at the same website.

To learn more about how you can participate in implementation of the full set of 39 recommendations, please visit: *http://environment.yale.edu/climate*.

ISBN 0-9707882-4-X

@ 2006 Yale School of Forestry & Environmental Studies

"We are now faced with the fact that tomorrow is today. We are con-fronted with the fierce urgency of now. *In this unfolding conundrum of life and history there is such a thing as being too late. Procrastination is still the thief of time. Life often leaves us standing bare, naked and dejected with a lost opportunity. The 'tide in the affairs of men' does not remain at the flood; it ebbs. We may cry out desperately for time to pause in her passage, but time is deaf to every plea and rushes on. Over the bleached bones and jumbled residue of numerous civilizations are writ-ten the pathetic words: 'Too late. . . .'"*

— Reverend Dr. Martin Luther King, Jr.

Table of Contents

Acknowledgements

Reverend and former Congressman Bob Edgar brought the house down at our Conference in Aspen when he recited the arresting Martin Luther King, Jr. quote that opens this report. But what was remarkable about our Conference was that nearly everyone there brought the house down at some point – in their unique ways. Whether through quiet moments of candor, piercing insights about dynamics in our society or intense debates, our remarkable participants delivered on the challenging mandate set before them.

Therefore our first and most important acknowledgement here is of that special group of Americans who joined us in Aspen. We thank them for their inspiring and successful modeling of the kind of dialogue our society needs to have more of, at all levels, on climate change and many other high-stakes issues facing our country and world – and for their ongoing contributions to implementing the action recommendations they devised.

Special thanks are due to our keynote speakers, who delivered inspiring remarks that illuminated the dynamics we were exploring in the Conference and also challenged the participants to work even harder to get at robust answers. Not only did they provide thoughtful speeches, they also stayed to engage thoroughly in the working group dialogues: Al Gore, John Kerry, Jim Leach and Jim Rogers.

I express my profound thanks to Gus Speth, the Dean of our School, who has brought extraordinary vision to everything he's done throughout his remarkable career of leadership on issues of environment and development – and continued that record in our collaboration on this Conference. Working with him on this and other endeavors is a professional and personal privilege. Without him, this Conference and the broader Yale "science-to-action" collaborative that has emerged from it would not have been possible.

Ellen Susman, Susan Crown and Marne Obernauer provided the original inspiration to exercise our School's convening capacity in this way, and to do so in Aspen, a special venue conducive to fresh thinking. Special thanks are due to Susan for providing key insights on our substantive goals and program, and for lending her knowledge of place as we scouted specific locations.

The following individuals shared invaluable insights in advance calls and meetings to make our mandate and program as engaging and worthwhile as possible: Ed Bass, Frances Beinecke, Peggy Bewkes, Steve

Curwood, Paul Gorman, Al Jubitz, Marty Kaplan, Larry Linden, Tom Lovejoy, Jonathan Rose, Steve Schneider, Peter Seligmann, Dave Skelly and Dick Wirthlin.

The following group of important thinkers provided outstanding panel presentations that crystallized key issues for our participants to take to their working groups: Stephen Bocking, Baruch Fischhoff, Melanie Green, Jon Krosnick, George Lakoff, Jane Lubchenco, Arthur Lupia, Steve Schneider and Richard Somerville. We acknowledge with gratitude Susan Crown, Bob Edgar, Al Franken, Susan Hassol and Tim Wirth for their stage-setting contributions.

Our working groups were chaired by an exceptional group of thoughtful leaders and academics: Jessica Catto, Marian Chertow, Richard Cizik, Dan Esty, David Fenton, Steve Kellert, Jonathan Lash, Debbie Levin, Jane Lubchenco and Jack Riggs.

All of the following enthusiastically and with great distinction performed the critical function of writing kickoff papers to set the table for our Conference: Frances Beinecke, Richard Cizik, Eileen Claussen, Kevin Coyle, Cornelia Dean, Bill Ellis, Brad Gentry, Melanie Green, Patricia Mastrandrea, Manik Roy and Steve Schneider.

The following talented individuals, most of them students at or alumni/ae of our School, did a great job as rapporteurs, capturing points from the meeting without which I could not have written this report, and also applying their keen judgment in advancing the dialogues. This group will continue to have a big impact on the climate change issue in the coming years: Maya Fischhoff, Kaitlin Gregg, Ann Grodnik, Kate Hamilton, Heather Kaplan, Virginia Lacy, Kelly Levin, Derek Murrow and Linda Shi.

The Conference and the ongoing implementation of this action plan would not be possible without the generosity of many individual donors and foundations who understood what we were trying to do and then did so much to help us shape it. Their continuing support and counsel are valued very highly by all of us at the School. We thank: Ed Bass, Frances Beinecke, Sally Brown, Jessica Catto, Susan Crown, Al Jubitz, Randy Katz, Larry Linden, Marne Obernauer, Jonathan Rose, Roger Sant, John Scurci, Ellen Susman, the Betsy and Jesse Fink Foundation, Hewlett Foundation, Kendall Foundation, W. L. Lyons Brown Foundation, Summit Foundation, Surdna Foundation and Winslow Foundation.

I express my deepest appreciation to Bill Ellis for his incisive guidance in sharpening the concept for this undertaking right from the outset and providing invaluable counsel throughout. His years as a corporate chieftain also proved indispensable in recruiting key participants.

We benefited enormously from Dan Esty's proven skills in inter-disciplinary research and practice as we refined our plans for the Conference. I also thank him for his guidance and vision in developing the research program of the Environmental Attitudes and Behavior Project, which I direct at the Yale Center on Environmental Law and Policy and which is becoming a hub for social science activity in furtherance of our Conference action plan. Melissa Goodall and the rest of the Center team have, under Dan Esty's leadership, built a dynamic enterprise.

The Conference and all the program activities around it, including this report, have been a true team effort, and I especially thank my talented and committed team at Yale for all they do every day: Chris Galvin, Jane Coppock, David DeFusco and Paul Smith. Chris deserves special recognition as the point-man on the Conference for performing his many demanding roles with aplomb and great interpersonal skill.

The School's Office of Development has been versatile and indispensable throughout this effort: Fred Regan brought a continual flow of important insights, and Eugénie Gentry, Mike Kiernan, Connie Royster and Michele Whitney were big contributors to our success. Deputy Dean Alan Brewster deserves appreciation for his steady hand and wise counsel, along with the Dean's office: Assistant Dean Pilar Montalvo, Catherine Marshall, Margot Massari and Sherry Ryan.

I express special gratitude to my good friends Baruch Fischhoff, Jon Krosnick and Arthur Lupia, extraordinarily gifted scholars who gave of their time and insight to help us think through our plan for melding academic and practitioner perspectives at this Conference and for creatively engaging the social sciences in grappling with the challenge of motivating societal action on climate change.

John Ehrmann, a nationally recognized facilitator in the environmental arena, provided insightful guidance as we designed our experimental format as well as on-site counsel, as did Jack Riggs of the Aspen Institute.

I thank Jason MacEachen, Doug Crawford and the rest of the Aspen Institute team for providing a wonderfully conducive environment for our Conference.

Since the Conference, a number of implementation activities, partnerships and presentations about the Conference findings have been underway with a wide range of special people, including David Blockstein, Erica Dawson, Bob Edgar, David Elisco, Anne Kelly, Mindy Lubber, Richard Somerville and Tim Wirth. Director of Alumni/ae Affairs Kath Schomaker has also engaged our School's talented alumni/ae into the implementation effort, and I'm grateful to her and to them.

Fred Strebeigh, a colleague at Yale, generously read this report and offered valuable comments, as did Dave DeFusco, Bill Ellis, Kate Hamilton and Gus Speth. Many thanks are due to Jane Coppock, Assistant Dean and Editor of the Yale F&ES Publication Series, and to Dorothy Scott and Eve Hornstein, for their excellent work and dedication in shepherding the report to publication.

I thank Jesse Fink and the team at MSM Capital Partners for the great collaboration and camaraderie as we put financial markets to work to mitigate climate change, especially: Mark Cirilli, Ramsay Ravenel, Mark Schwartz, Martin Whittaker, Ryan Franco, Charles Byrd, Dan Donovan, Patty Nolan and Tanya Boland. My mother Susan and stepfather Wendell Fletcher have my heartfelt love and appreciation. I express my deepest love to my wife, Deborah Smith, and children – Jordy, Eli and Isabelle – for everything, including their forbearance as I have diverted so much time to this consuming work on climate change. I hold out hope that these efforts, along with those of so many others, will have an effect on improving my children's lives and those of their contemporaries.

Daniel R. Abbasi
March 2006

Foreword

James Gustave Speth
Dean, Yale School of Forestry & Environmental Studies

Despite credible forecasts and warnings from the scientific community about climate change for a quarter of a century, greenhouse gas emissions have continued to grow, signals of human-induced climate change have clearly emerged, and a preponderance of scientists studying the issue project more adverse consequences to come unless stronger actions are taken.

Yet a substantial political gulf persists between those advocating such actions and those opposed. Sir David King, Chief Scientific Advisor to the British government, wrote in *Science* in 2004 that "climate change is the most severe problem that we are facing today – more serious even than the threat of terrorism." He called for "early, well-planned action" leading to the developed economies cutting their greenhouse gas emissions by 60 percent below 1990 levels by 2050, and warned that "delaying action for decades, or even years, is not a serious option."[*]

But public and policy-maker commitment to action of this seriousness remains elusive indeed. The U.S. government, citing remaining scientific uncertainties, economic costs, and the unfairness of a global regulatory regime that excludes the developing world, has rejected the Kyoto Protocol and largely refrained from positive international engagement on the issue. Today there are signs everywhere that the climate issue is beginning to gain traction, but the gap between climate science and climate policy and action remains huge.

What explains this gap? Is climate change merely one instance of a larger problem, namely, the expanding gulf between the increasingly scientific and technical content of public policy issues on the one hand, and the declining public understanding of science and technology on the other? Good environmental science and forecasting are absolutely necessary but, it would appear, far from sufficient. If we want science to affect real-world decisions and events, how can we best address the barriers that lie between good science and effective policy and action?

On October 6-8, 2005, the Yale School of Forestry & Environmental Studies brought a group of 110 leading thinkers and actors together in

---

[*] David A. King, "Climate Change Science: Adapt, Mitigate or Ignore," Science, Vol. 303, 9 January 2004: 176-77.

Aspen, Colorado, for a conference entitled "Climate Change: From Science to Action." Our goal was to examine the gap between climate science and climate policy and action, with a particular focus on public understanding as a key intervening variable. Many have validated this as an area needing more focus and action. For example, General Electric CEO Jeffrey Immelt and World Resources Institute President Jonathan Lash asserted in a Washington Post Op-Ed in mid-2005 that the key missing ingredient in tackling our energy and climate challenges is a "strong dose of public will."

Reflecting our belief that society's response to climate change is an interactive and complex equation, we invited a diverse cross-section of participants representing eight societal "domains": Science, News Media, Religion & Ethics, Politics, Entertainment & Advertising, Education, Business & Finance and Environmentalists & Civil Society. We created eight working groups and asked each to develop:

- diagnoses of how their respective domains may have contributed to the gap between climate science and policy and action (due to such factors as occupational identities, norms, practices, incentive systems and others); and

- ideas and initiatives to help close the gap, both through action steps within their respective domains and new or enhanced cross-domain collaborations.

To complement the working group meetings, we engaged numerous members of Congress, political leaders, and world-class academics on the role of science in social change theory and practice, human psychology and climate change, and the state of climate change science.

The event did not presuppose that the science of climate change or any other issue is monolithic or infallible. While we do believe that key elements of the scientific consensus on climate change have not been effectively communicated and understood, we also evaluated factors that complicate the authority of science as an objective and universal guide to action: its complexity, lack of transparency, and resistance to local input. We discussed these concerns, as well as solutions that could democratize or open up the scientific process itself in ways that might engender a more scientifically literate and engaged public.

Given that climate change is a global problem, why did we focus on the United States? There have been many important meetings looking at other countries' emissions profiles and climate change policies, as well as at how the international negotiations might evolve beyond the Kyoto

Protocol (whose emissions obligations end in 2012). Our meeting sought to avoid duplicating those meetings or efforts. Rather, our focus in Aspen was on what many regard as the most important outlier in the world today regarding climate change action: the United States.

The meeting also sought to address broader themes beyond those related to climate change. Climate change was our focal case and was front and center in our dialogues, but we also sought to shed light on the broader issue of the role of science in a deliberative democracy: How can citizens best engage on the full range of issues with a high scientific and technical content? In this context, we discussed whether and how climate is a distinctive case relative to other environmental or societal problems.

This report was prepared by conference director Dan Abbasi, Associate Dean for Public Affairs and Strategic Initiatives at our School, based on our discussions at Aspen. Dean Abbasi begins in Part I with an admirable analysis based on the diagnostic findings and recommendations of the working groups, and in Part II he describes in full the 39 key recommendations to emerge from the Conference.

The conferees were not asked to seek consensus. Therefore the contents of this report should not be construed as reflecting consensus or sign-off. Many of the diagnostic insights and action items reported here did gain a significant measure of support among the conferees, while others are the input of smaller groups. In some instances, the logic of an insight or dialogue from the Conference is extended to fashion a new idea. Our intention in this report is to include a wide range of key ideas, without regard to their breadth of support, and to allow the readers (and potential implementers) to apply their own judgment in evaluating their quality, feasibility and value.

I believe the report presents an enormously valuable agenda for further research and, especially, action. We saw in Aspen a clear recognition that society's response to the climate change issue will depend on broadening the circle of engagement and devising innovative new collaborations and partnerships across all sectors and communities. We hope that readers of this report will participate actively in such endeavors.

We at Yale's environment school anticipate playing a role in catalyzing the implementation of selected action items and in monitoring progress toward fulfilling the action items outlined on our website (*http://environment.yale.edu/climate*). Clearly, many individuals and institutions will need to step forward and assume leadership roles in making these initiatives happen, either by funding or leading their implementation. Climate change is one of the great challenges of our time, and, as this report underscores, there is not only much to be done, but an urgency to take steps that have been too long delayed.

Executive Summary

Why has the robust and compelling body of climate change science not had a greater impact on action, especially in the United States?

From the policy-making level down to personal voting and purchasing decisions, our actions as Americans have not been commensurate with the threat as characterized by mainstream science.

Meaningful pockets of entrepreneurial initiative have emerged at the city and state level, in the business sector, and in "civil society" more generally. But we remain far short of undertaking the emissions reductions that scientists say are required if we are to forestall dangerous interference in the climate system on which civilization depends.

In late 2005, the Yale School of Forestry & Environmental Studies convened 110 leaders and thinkers in Aspen, Colorado, and asked them to diagnose the reasons for this posited action shortfall and to generate recommendations to address it. This report discusses findings from that gathering of extraordinary Americans.

Part I of this report is a synthesis that highlights eight selected themes from the Conference, each of which relates to a cluster of diagnoses, recommendations, and important lines of debate or inquiry. Part II describes the diagnoses and 39 recommendations from the eight working groups. The eight themes and ten of the most prominent recommendations are spotlighted below.

THEMES FROM PART I

Scientific Disconnects

We are only aware of climate change as a human-induced phenomenon because of science. Given this scientific "origin," the default tendency of those who seek to propagate the issue throughout society is to preserve its scientific trappings: by retaining scientific terminology, relying on scientists as lead messengers, and adhering to norms of scientific conservatism. Such practices can cause profound disconnects in how society interprets and acts on the climate change issue, and they deserve our remedial attention.

From Science to Values

Given the challenges with propagating the science of climate change throughout society, many people now favor shifting to a values-based approach to motivating action on the issue. Religious communities, in particular, are increasingly adopting the climate change issue in fulfillment of their stewardship values. Yet a science-to-values repositioning, whether religious or secular, carries risks of its own that need to be understood and managed.

Packaging Climate Change as an Energy Issue

Frustrated by the inability of climate change to break through as an urgent public concern, many believe it is best to finally admit that the issue cannot stand on its own. Climate change can be packaged with other issues that have generated more public concern to date – and energy security is a leading candidate. This is a promising strategy, but it also risks deemphasizing climate change mitigation as an explicit societal priority precisely when it needs to move up on the list.

Incentives

It is tempting to reduce the challenge of promoting action on climate change to matters of communications and strategic positioning. Yet this will usually only take us part of the way. Translating awareness into action depends on identifying – and selectively modifying – the deeper incentive structures at play in our society. Harnessing climate change objectives to the material incentives to modify energy supply and use patterns is an important part of the equation. But a more thorough domain-by-domain analysis of career and organizational incentives yields additional levers for fashioning a broad-based set of strategies.

Diffusion of Responsibility

After evaluating the incentives operating within each of the eight societal domains represented at the Conference, it is now worthwhile to reassemble the pieces and identify patterns cutting across them. Doing so yields the sobering insight that we are experiencing diffusion of responsibility on climate change. While no single individual or domain can plausibly be expected to take solitary charge on this encompassing problem, many who could assume leadership appear to think it is someone else's prerogative, or obligation, to do so. The result: a leadership vacuum.

The Affliction of Partisanship

Climate change is a partisan issue in today's America. The policy stalemate in Washington, D.C. has left those committed to action uncertain about whether a partisan or bipartisan strategy is more likely to succeed going forward. For all its direct costs, partisanship has also had profound spillover effects, chilling public engagement on climate change throughout our society and compelling many people to take sides instead of collaborating to craft policies and actions as warranted by the science.

Setting Goals

Those working to promote societal action on climate change need to do a better job of formulating goals that are capable of promoting convergent strategies by dispersed and often uncoordinated actors, and commensurate with a real solution to the problem. In order to guide and motivate needed actions, these goals should be generated collaboratively, scientifically calibrated, quantifiable, trackable and easily expressible. They should include not only emissions targets but also, given the crucial importance of "public will," attitudinal targets.

Leveraging the Social Sciences

The facts of climate change cannot be left to speak for themselves. They must be actively communicated with the right words, in the right dosages, packaged with narrative storytelling that is based rigorously on reality, personalized with human faces, made vivid through visual imagery – and delivered by the right messengers. Doing this will require that climate change communications go from being a data-poor to a data-rich arena. Social science methods have not been adequately applied to date – and that must change, given the stakes.

TEN RECOMMENDATIONS FROM PART II

Part II of this report describes in detail the diagnoses of the science-action gap that were conducted by each of the eight working groups, and subsequently refined in mixed-group formats. It also lays out each of the 39 recommendations, providing supporting rationales and in some cases points of debate. The recommendations represent the output of concentrated dialogue among a thoughtful and diverse group of Americans, but sign-off should not be construed, as they were not submitted to a vote or any consensus-building procedures. The following constitute ten of the most prominent recommendations to emerge.

Recommendation #1: Create a new "bridging institution" to actively seek out key business, religious, political, and civic leaders and the media and deliver to them independent, reliable and credible scientific information about climate change (including natural and economic sciences).

Recommendation #7: Educate the gatekeepers (i.e., editors). In order to improve the communication of climate science in the news media, foster a series of visits and conferences whereby respected journalists and editors informed on climate change can speak to their peer editors. The objective is to have those who can credibly talk about story ideas and craft reach out to their peers about how to cover the climate change issue with appropriate urgency, context, and journalistic integrity.

Recommendation #11: Religious leaders and communities must recognize the scale, urgency and moral dimension of climate change, and the ethical unacceptability of any action that damages the quality and viability of life on Earth, particularly for the poor and most vulnerable.

Recommendation #20: Design and execute a "New Vision for Energy" campaign to encourage a national market-based transition to alternative energy sources. Harness multiple messages tailored to different audiences that embed the climate change issue in a larger set of co-benefit narratives, such as: reducing U.S. dependency on Middle East oil (national security); penetrating global export markets with American innovations (U.S. stature); boosting U.S. job growth (jobs); and cutting local air pollution (health).

Recommendation #25: Create a new overarching communications entity or project to design and execute a well-financed public education campaign on climate change science and its implications. This multi-faceted campaign would leverage the latest social science findings concerning attitude formation and change on climate change, and would use all available media in an effort to disseminate rigorously accurate information, and to counter disinformation in real time.

Recommendation #26: Undertake systematic and rigorous projects to test the impact of environmental communications in all media (e.g., advertising, documentary, feature film) on civic engagement, public opinion and persuasive outcomes. Use these to inform new creative work on multi-media climate change communications.

Recommendation #28: Improve K-12 students' understanding of climate change by promoting it as a standards-based content area within science curricula and incorporating it into other disciplinary curricula and teacher certification standards. Use the occasion of the state reviews of science standards for this purpose, which are being prompted by the states' need to comply with the Fall 2007 start of high-stakes science testing under the No Child Left Behind Act.

Recommendation #29: Organize a grassroots educational campaign to create local narratives around climate change impacts and solutions, while mobilizing citizen engagement and action. Kick the campaign off with a National Climate Week that would recur on an annual basis.

Recommendation #33: The Business & Finance working group at the Conference composed an eight-principle framework, and proposed that it be disseminated broadly to trade associations and individual business leaders (especially at the CEO and board level) as a set of clear and feasible actions that businesses can and should take on climate change.

Recommendation #36: Create a broad-based Climate Action Leadership Council of 10-12 recognizable and senior eminent leaders from all key national sectors and constituencies to serve as an integrating mechanism for developing and delivering a cohesive message to society about the seriousness of climate change and the imperative of taking action. The Council would include leaders from business, labor, academia, government, the NGO sector, the professions (medicine, law, and public health) and community leaders. They would be chosen on the basis of their credibility within their respective communities, but also across society at large.

To learn more about how you can participate in implementation of the full set of 39 recommendations, please visit: *http://environment.yale.edu/climate*

Part I

Matching Up to the Perfect Problem

INTRODUCTION

Why has the robust and compelling body of climate change science not had a greater impact on action, especially in the United States?

From the policy-making level down to personal voting and purchasing decisions, our actions as Americans have not been commensurate with the threat as characterized by mainstream science.

Meaningful pockets of entrepreneurial initiative have emerged at the city and state level, in the business sector, and in "civil society" more generally. But we remain far short of undertaking the emissions reductions that scientists say are required if we are to forestall dangerous interference in the climate system on which our civilization depends.

The problem of climate change is almost perfectly designed to test the limits of any modern society's capacity for response – one might even call it the "perfect problem" for its uniquely daunting confluence of forces:

> ➤ complex and inaccessible scientific content;

> ➤ a substantial (and uncertain) time lag between cause and effect;

> ➤ inertia in all the key drivers of the problem, from demographic growth to long-lived energy infrastructure to ingrained daily habits at the household level;

> ➤ psychological barriers that complicate apprehension and processing of the issue, due in part to its perceived remoteness in time and place;

> ➤ partisan, cultural, and other filters that cause social discounting or obfuscation of the threat;

> ➤ motivational obstacles, especially the futility associated with what is perhaps the quintessential "collective action problem" of our time;

> ➤ mismatches between the global, cross-sectoral scope of the climate change issue and the jurisdiction, focus, and capacity of existing institutions;

> ➤ a set of hard-wired incentives, career and otherwise, that inhibit focused attention and action on the issue.

In late 2005, the Yale School of Forestry & Environmental Studies convened 110 leaders and thinkers in Aspen, Colorado, and asked them to develop their own diagnosis of the gap between science and action from the standpoint of their respective societal "domains": Science,

News Media, Religion & Ethics, Politics, Entertainment & Advertising, Education, Business & Finance and Environmentalists & Civil Society.

This report discusses the findings reached at that gathering of extraordinary Americans.

Part I is a synthesis essay that describes selected themes from the Conference, each reflecting an informal post hoc grouping of diagnoses and recommendations. Rather than adhere strictly to reporting on ideas generated at the Conference, original commentary is offered on given topics and context is provided for others. In a few instances, caution and further research are advised before undertaking implementation of certain recommendations. The author's post-Conference vantage point allowed for detection of patterns and themes across the findings (e.g., diffusion of responsibility or the "four paradoxes of urgency"). However, this also means that the reader should not construe sign-off by the Conference participants on any particular points, even though all were inspired in some measure by their various and generous contributions to the dialogue.

Part II of the report is a group-by-group description of the diagnoses and recommendations developed at the Conference, although the approach here, too, remains inescapably interpretive since the source material was rapporteur notes from the deliberations, not tapes or literal transcripts. We refrained from recording the event in order to encourage candid dialogue. The reader should not construe sign-off by the participants on Part II either, though their comments on an earlier draft have been incorporated.

Some readers may prefer to skip past the synthesis essay in Part I and go straight to the meat of the recommendations in Part II, or even to the summary list of recommendations in the back of the report. Others may value the narrative walk-through in Part I as a thematic foundation for the detail in Part II.

Four Contextual Points

➢ First, this report does not review the science of climate change. It begins with the premise that the science is sufficiently sound and concerning to warrant a focus on the next question, which is how society absorbs, interprets, propagates and ultimately acts on that science. For those seeking authoritative reviews and updates on the science, here are a few recommendations:

• The National Academy of Sciences' Marian Koshland Science Museum website offers an accessible primer on climate change. *www.koshland-science-museum.org/exhibitgcc*

- Sir John Houghton's book, *Global Warming: The Complete Briefing*, now in its third edition, is a highly regarded review of the science.

- The Intergovernmental Panel on Climate Change (IPCC) website offers a wealth of authoritative scientific information, including the IPCC's three major assessment reports, as well as speeches, slide presentations, workshop proceedings, and supporting technical papers. *www.ipcc.ch*

- The U.S. National Assessment Synthesis team, under the auspices of the U.S. Government's Global Change Research Program, produced a 2000 report entitled "Climate Change Impacts on the United States." *www.usgcrp.gov/usgcrp/nacc*

- Real Climate is a rich and topical website written by working climate scientists for the interested public and journalists that aims "to provide a quick response to developing stories and provide the context sometimes missing in mainstream commentary." *www.realclimate.org*

- The Pew Center on Global Climate Change website includes basic and topical information on climate change science, and links to many government agency websites on the issue, including the data-rich website of the National Oceanic and Atmospheric Administration. *www.pewclimate.org/global-warming-basics*

➢ Second, this report does not constitute a policy roadmap on climate change in the United States. While the issue of emissions targets and pathways is briefly discussed in the section on goal-setting at the end of Part I, the predominant focus here is on public understanding, will, and motivation as a *precursor* to policy and other forms of action. Others are doing brilliant and intricate policy work on how we should – if public and political will enables it – create a fair and effective program in the United States to mitigate climate change, whether through a nationwide cap-and-trade system or some other framework.

➢ Third, while we assembled a diverse group at the Conference, the reader should be informed that it was not fully representative of America. Our goal was to generate creative diagnoses and fresh solutions in a reasonably intimate setting, not to fashion a broader societal consensus on site. We had geographic, ethnic, occupational, religious, and sectoral gaps, and therefore in no way presume that our event could be considered a true national summit on climate change. That said, we believe our model for candid cross-domain dialogue could usefully be built upon and expanded in future meetings.

➤ Fourth, we adopted a problem-driven orientation in our Conference as a springboard to creative thinking about new solutions, and that approach is sustained in this report. Accordingly, many pages are devoted to what's *not* happening and why, which then leads into discussions about what needs to happen next. This leaves less room for celebrating the considerable progress already underway on climate change in the United States. This should not be read as a defeatist tone. Perhaps the most hopeful sign that we are on the right track is when our society engages in candid, reality-based dialogue about a problem, because that is the best foundation for solutions that will really work. Optimism is more implicit than explicit in this approach – but it is assuredly a critical ingredient.

Signs That Action Is Advancing

References to various success stories underway are interspersed throughout this report, in part to caution against duplicating them and also to suggest that they be built upon and augmented wherever possible. Before starting in, however, it is worthwhile to highlight in one place a few examples of the range of climate change action underway today in the United States. This is intended to be illustrative, not comprehensive. It should hearten those committed to bridging the gap between science and action. Then we can fasten our seatbelts and plunge, together, into the maw of the problem and discuss how best to address it. Here are some highlights:

➤ **Senate resolution.** The U.S. Senate approved a resolution on June 22, 2005 (by a 53-44 vote) resolving that: "It is the sense of the Senate that Congress should enact a comprehensive and effective national program of mandatory market-based limits and incentives on greenhouse gases that slow, stop and reverse the growth of such emissions. . . ." Bipartisan legislation is now being crafted along these lines, and a conference on Capitol Hill is planned for April 2006 to assess the options. (Prospects for near-term action in the House of Representatives appear less promising.)

➢ **Mayoral pledge.** Mayors of 219 U.S. cities, representing 43.7 million Americans, have pledged to meet city-level goals consistent with the Kyoto Protocol, by signing the U.S. Mayors' Climate Protection Agreement, an initiative led by Seattle Mayor Greg Nickels (*www.ci.seattle.wa.us/mayor/climate*).

➢ **Advertising.** The Ad Council, which produced one of the highest-recall advertisements of all time in 1971, popularly known as "The Crying Indian," launched in late March 2006 a major TV, print and radio advertising campaign on climate change, in cooperation with Environmental Defense and the Robertson Foundation. It will focus both on the urgency of the issue and on providing steps that individuals can take to conserve energy and lower their emissions (*www.fightglobalwarming.com*).

➢ **Regional Greenhouse Gas Initiative (RGGI).** The Governors of seven Northeastern and Mid-Atlantic states signed a Memorandum of Understanding in December 2005 to create a regional cap-and-trade plan to reduce emissions from power plants. RGGI will also provide credits for emissions reductions achieved outside of the electricity sector (*www.rggi.org*).

➢ **Popular media.** Fox News aired a 1-hour special in late 2005 that played against its conservative reputation entitled: "The Heat Is On: The Case of Global Warming." HBO will air in April 2006 a global warming special entitled "Too Hot Not to Handle." Turner Broadcasting System took on the Herculean task of making global warming funny in a 2-hour comedy special called "Earth to America, which aired in November 2005. The CBS Series *60 Minutes* did a segment on the Arctic Climate Impact Assessment in February 2006.

➢ **California.** In June 2005, Governor Arnold Schwarzenegger committed to reduce California's greenhouse gases to 1990 levels by 2020 and 80 percent by 2050. California passed the first law in the nation to cut automobile emissions of greenhouse gases (22 percent by 2012 and 30 percent by 2016), though an automaker legal challenge is pending. New York adopted the same standard on November 9, 2005, and other states are following. In February 2006, the California Public Utilities Commission announced plans to cap greenhouse gas emissions from the state's power plants. California, Washington and Oregon are cooperating on a strategy to reduce GHG emissions called the West Coast Governors' Global Warming Initiative (*www.ef.org/westcoastclimate*).

➤ **Other state action.** Twenty-eight states now have climate action plans, including nine with statewide emissions targets. Twenty-two states and the District of Columbia have mandated that electric utilities generate a specified amount of electricity from renewable sources – known as Renewable Portfolio Standards (*www.pewclimate.org/policy_center/state_policy*).

➤ **Corporate commitments.** Scores of U.S. companies continue to make and execute commitments to reduce greenhouse gases through a variety of governmental and NGO-based voluntary programs and registries, ranging from the Chicago Climate Exchange (*www.chicagoclimatex.com*) to the Pew Center's Business Environmental Leadership Council, with 41 members representing $2 trillion in market capitalization (*www.pewclimate.org/companies_leading_the_way_belc*).

➤ **Institutional investors.** Investors managing over $2.7 trillion in assets and coordinating their efforts through the Investor Network on Climate Risk released a 10-point action plan on May 10, 2005, calling on U.S. companies, Wall Street firms, and the SEC to provide investors with comprehensive analysis and disclosure about the financial risks presented by climate change (*www.incr.org*).

➤ **Civil society.** Civil society is increasingly active on climate change, ranging from the diverse Apollo Alliance coalition on clean energy (*www.apolloalliance.org*) to the 25 x 25 initiative to develop farm-based sources capable of supplying 25 percent of U.S. energy by 2025 (*www.agenergy.info*). The new Evangelical Climate Initiative issued a "Call to Action" in February 2006 (*www.christiansandclimate.org*).

➤ **Energy action.** Energy Action, a North American coalition of 30 student and youth clean energy organizations, was recently launched (*www.energyaction.net*). Among other activities, Energy Action is advancing the Campus Climate Challenge, a grassroots effort to secure emissions reductions on over 500 high school and college campuses (*http://campusclimatechallenge.org*).

➤ **Rethinking oil dependence.** There is a growing convergence between those who are concerned about the security implications of U.S. oil dependence and those focused on reducing oil use to mitigate climate change. In his 2006 State of the Union address, President Bush added his weight to those concerned about

America's current energy use by saying that America is "addicted to oil" and calling for increasing research into alternative energy sources. The President has, however, continued to oppose regulation of greenhouse gases domestically and engagement in international negotiations to cap emissions.

Encouraged by this range of progress, we now proceed to discuss some of the key challenges still ahead, and ways to address them.

SCIENTIFIC DISCONNECTS

We are only aware of climate change as a human-induced phenomenon because of science. Given this scientific "origin," the default tendency of those who seek to propagate the issue throughout society is to preserve its scientific trappings: by retaining scientific terminology, relying on scientists as lead messengers, and adhering to norms of scientific conservatism. Such practices can cause profound disconnects in how society interprets and acts on the climate change issue, and they deserve our remedial attention.

Climate change is a quintessentially scientific issue in that, without the scientific method, we would not be aware of it. We would not be talking about human causality. We would not be assembling the disparate data points from around the globe and seeing their total significance. Yet when an issue is scientifically defined, it is not always clear how long it should remain so as it is propagated throughout society.

Scientific Word Choice and Metrics

We have not yet found the right words to communicate about climate change, arguably including the name of the phenomenon itself. Is it appropriate to factor marketability and motivational power into the very naming of a scientific phenomenon, or is that the sacrosanct province of the scientists? Scientists appear to prefer the term climate change because it is more encompassing – allowing for non-temperature effects such as precipitation, chemical alteration of the oceans, as well as a patchwork of warming and cooling regions.

Polls of the public, meanwhile, indicate that the phrase "global warming" is more attention-getting and unsettling to people than "climate change," even though "warming" on its own has a pleasant, welcoming ring. Alternative terms have been proposed, including "climate disruption," "runaway warming," or "catastrophic warming."

Few Americans can distinguish the meanings of weather and climate. Since they routinely experience rapid weather changes, why should a change in climate be any more concerning? Longstanding models of balance and equilibrium in ecosystems have largely been superceded by new ones emphasizing constant change, chaos, multiple equilibria and amplifications of small causes into large effects. Given all this, and the historical evidence of major climate changes prior to the onset of human influences (from the Cretaceous Thermal Maximum to the Permo Carboniferous Glaciation), it can sound like a fool's errand to stop climate change, or any other change for that matter.

Nonetheless, those seeking to advance societal action on the issue appear to have resigned themselves to perpetuating the scientifically preferred term "climate change," but should they? It is arguably not too late to revisit the naming conundrum if we place sufficient value on the specific goal of translating science to action.

Apart from its naming, the issue has been loaded up with an impenetrable construct of jargon – ranging from the scientists' "positive feedback loops" or "positive radiative forcing" ("positive" in these cases actually refers to something bad) to the policy-makers' tradable emissions permits denominated in "tons" of carbon dioxide-equivalent (to the average American, "tons" presumably connote elephants more than invisible air molecules). Scientists say "anthropogenic" when "man-made" would be more widely understood.

The impact of scientific conservatism on word choice can be seen in the varying interpretations of the Intergovernmental Panel on Climate Change's (IPCC) Second Assessment Report in 1995. The most widely reported phrase from that report was that "the balance of evidence suggests a discernible human influence on global climate." To those predisposed to concern about the issue, this statement equated to a smoking gun. After all, thousands of scientists laboring in distinct countries and sub-disciplines had come to a consensus that the signal of human impact could now be distinguished from the noise of natural variability.

Yet in common parlance, discernible implies tiny, or at least barely detectable. Can the layperson be expected to hear this smallish word and immediately thrust the issue to the top of his or her agenda of concerns? Incidentally, the IPCC's Third Assessment Report in 2001 strengthened the language about the human role, saying: "There is new and stronger evidence that most of the warming observed over the last 50 years is attributable to human activities." But the point stands: word choices at any given moment in the unfolding communication of an issue can be interpreted differently based on the prior dispositions of the person hearing the message.

A pervasive, and probably underestimated, problem in scientific-public discourse is the nearly universal use of the scientifically preferred Celsius measure for temperature in communicating about climate change, even though Fahrenheit remains the ubiquitous measure in the U.S. and the only one to which average Americans can relate. This default usage of Centigrade (the Celsius measure) is problematic also because the numbers are smaller and the magnitude of current or projected warming is therefore perceptually diminished. So the IPCC's projected range of a 1.4 – 5.8° Centigrade rise in temperature by 2100 sounds notably smaller than its 2.5 – 10.4° Fahrenheit equivalent.

Choose Your Consequence

For those aiming to raise public awareness of the projected consequences of climate change, a laundry list is available: sea-level rise, extreme weather events, droughts and water shortages, agricultural and food risks, infectious disease, ecosystem loss, species extinction, and others.

The Biblical quality of these consequences – floods, droughts, plagues – has often been assumed to be an advantage in getting people's attention, even though the associations with divine wrath may also promote a sense of human futility.

An intuitive overview suggests, moreover, that many of the climate change risks may not be as viscerally unsettling to people as one might think. Sea-level rise may be perceived as inherently geological and long-term, even if accelerations lie ahead from unexpectedly rapid ice sheet melting (new satellite observations reported in the journal *Science* in February 2006 show that Greenland's glaciers are sliding toward the sea almost twice as fast as previously thought). The spread of climate-sensitive diseases to new latitudes and elevations sounds troubling, but disease risk is a probabilistic phenomenon and many people appear to like their chances in such situations. Food scarcity from disrupted agriculture and threats to drinking water may cut closest to home, but at least in the industrial world, the image of plentiful grocery stores is so deeply imprinted that it may be difficult to shake it loose even if a particular projection warrants it.

The fact is that there is surprisingly little hard evidence about which of the many climate change related risks are of greatest concern to the American population. The risk perception and communications fields have largely focused elsewhere (e.g., seat belt usage, drunk driving, STDs, cancer screening), typically on issues of personal behavior rather than daunting collective action problems like climate change. And the major survey organizations rarely probe these depths, instead going only so far as asking whether Americans think global warming is a serious or very serious problem as a whole.

Even if we had better data, one may ask whether it is scientifically legitimate to select some consequences above others for motivational purposes, when the science encompasses all of them. If an important goal is to translate science to action, however, such choices may simply need to be made. Communications can be constructed that remain faithful to the natural sciences, while doing much more to reflect our advancing understanding of how human beings assess risks.

Communicating the Risks or the Solutions

There is, as well, a more basic question, discussed a great deal at the Conference, of whether communicating the risks associated with climate change to Americans is the correct route to go in the first place. Many contend that it is time to discontinue "scare-mongering" and alarmism, and instead portray a hopeful vision of solutions that will create jobs and pump up the economy. Those seeking to advance action will likely need to communicate both consequences and solutions. Finding the right balance and sequence to promote action commensurate with the science is a task that will need to draw not just on the natural sciences but also on the social sciences (see more on this theme later in Part I).

Meanwhile, many at the Conference intuitively recognized the potential value of better understanding and communicating local impacts of climate change so that Americans would grasp what this issue could mean for their well-being and that of their children. Recognizing that this is partly a function of the available science, Conference Recommendation #2 calls for research priorities on climate change to be more responsive to society's information and decision-making needs, including acceleration of ongoing efforts to observe and model local impacts at greater resolution levels.

Scientific Conservatism Meets Today's Weather

Weather extremes and anomalies increasingly provoke societal discussion about climate change. For example, the unusually warm East Coast January in 2006 appears, anecdotally at least, to have increased the general public chatter about climate change. At the time of our Conference in the fall of 2005, Hurricanes Katrina and Rita were utmost in the public's mind.

Such events present what has become a recurring dilemma: Should those seeking to prompt action on climate change opportunistically exploit the spike in public concern? Or should they remain scientifically conservative and seek to disabuse people of the notion that individual weather events or seasons, alone, confirm that human-induced climate change is happening?

If such public concerns are treated as a "teachable moment," this may offer fleeting gains in the public's propensity to act, while also incurring a significant risk that when the local weather turns again, concern will dissipate and even sustain a backlash.

Distinguished University of California scientist Richard Somerville discussed the recent hurricanes at our Conference and agreed to paraphrase his comments for this report. He writes that:

> "A warmer climate means that, statistically, hurricanes may be stronger, on average. It does not mean we can definitely prove that any particular hurricane owes its strength to climate change, only that the odds of strong hurricanes have gone up. There is persuasive scientific evidence from observations, theory and models that higher sea surface temperatures should and apparently do increase the duration and the average maximum intensity, but not the frequency, of hurricanes. There has clearly been a big observed increase in the duration of hurricanes and in their average maximum wind speeds in recent decades. The number of Category Four and Five hurricanes globally has nearly doubled since 1970.
>
> We know that hurricanes are highly variable, no two are alike, and next year's hurricane season might be very different from this year's. It is our natural inclination to wait a few more years, observe more hurricanes, improve our theories and models, until we have an airtight case to present. Science is inherently self-correcting, and later research can always confirm, extend or disprove earlier research. Nevertheless, the best current research tells us that all the oceans have recently warmed substantially, that human activities are the primary cause of that warming, that an increase in the average intensity of hurricanes is the expected result, and that we have indeed observed a remarkable increase in the numbers of the strongest hurricanes. No amount of waffling over probabilities and statistics can obscure these sobering results."

This is an example of clear scientific communication, which is more the exception than the norm in our society (and of course even this passage, for all its admirable clarity, is too long to be delivered as a sound bite on the TV news). Due to the inherent variability of the climate system, few if any specific weather events will ever meet the unrealistic standard of serving as definitive proof of climate change. But many can be described as "consistent with" or "indicative of" what we expect to see now or in the near future under a disrupted climate. And, as Somerville illustrates, such language can be used to describe how specific events fit – or don't fit – a larger pattern.

In this spirit, a number of our Conference recommendations seek to improve the scientific literacy and communications capabilities of those best positioned to portray this high-stakes issue to Americans. Together, they promote ways for our journalists and editors, teachers, business leaders, religious leaders, TV weathercasters and the scientists themselves to have access to timely information that puts today's weather events into context using clear language.

Such events present what has become a recurring dilemma: Should those seeking to prompt action on climate change opportunistically exploit the spike in public concern? Or should they remain scientifically conservative and seek to disabuse people of the notion that individual weather events or seasons, alone, confirm that human-induced climate change is happening?

The Conference participants did not have time to craft any particular turns of phrase, but instead called for new institutions, capacity-building, training and even coordinated advertising initiatives that will evaluate these issues with great care and ultimately supply our society's communicators with language that is scientifically accurate without being too reticent or opaque to gain wider notice and comprehension.

One metaphor that may bear expanded usage is that of the "human fingerprint," a clear way of summarizing the meaning of a flourishing body of research collectively known as "detection and attribution studies." This is a key ingredient often missing from the news coverage of observable effects, namely lucid and concise explanations of how scientists can, with increasing confidence, attribute the causes of observed effects to human rather than natural causes. Studies of the temperatures at different levels of the atmosphere (e.g., tropospheric warming versus stratospheric cooling), decreases in the day-night temperature range and land-sea temperature differences, among many others, provide mutually reinforcing observations that together distinguish the human fingerprint from natural causes such as solar or volcanic activity.

Nobody should expect Americans to cozy up for bedtime reading of such studies, but more can be done to translate these findings for broader accessibility. Exploring how this should be done is part of the task of the "bridging institution" called for in Recommendation #1. In short, this institution would be a science-led effort to use all media, the Internet, and other opportunities to translate and direct the scientific results on climate change in journals such as *Science, Nature, Climatic Change* and elsewhere to the alert, reachable public.

Observable versus Projected Impacts

All the above suggests the potential value of stepping back to a more basic question: What balance should those seeking to prompt action strike between information about currently observable consequences of climate change and the highly concerning projections of future impacts?

Popular news coverage about climate change is strongly biased toward highlighting emerging evidence that climate change is or may be underway *today*, namely, retreating glaciers and melting icecaps, European heat-waves and floods, and record-breaking hurricane seasons. Such stories are tangible and vivid. They counteract the public interpretation of the issue as a long-term threat only, and help to make it newsworthy. And yet coverage of observable climate change may be the toughest scientific turf to play on since it is relatively more uncertain than projections of future changes likely to transpire if we remain on our current emissions trajectory.

What balance should those seeking to prompt action strike between information about currently observable consequences of climate change and the highly concerning projections of future impacts?

This may seem paradoxical: Shouldn't something here *today* be more certain than something coming *tomorrow*? In fact, we have made major progress in identifying the human fingerprint evident today and distinguishing it from the natural variability of the climate. Yet our confidence in projections of future impacts, assuming continued increases in emissions, is still relatively greater. This point is encapsulated in a summary table in the Intergovernmental Panel on Climate Change's Third Assessment Report from 2001 showing the scientists' relative confidence levels in many climate change phenomena – ranging from drought risk to peak cyclone intensities to the frequency and maximum temperature of hot days. The confidence level associated with each phenomenon's occurrence is shown to be equal or higher when considering future projections over the 21st century than retrospective observations from the latter half of the 20th century. To the extent that future projections contain uncertainty – and they do – the scientific debates center on how rapid and severe the changes will be, not whether they will transpire if we continue emitting greenhouse gases at growing rates.

And what do our future emissions look like? To date, humanity has increased the concentration of the primary greenhouse gas, carbon dioxide, in our atmosphere by just over 30 percent (i.e., from approximately 280 parts per million in the pre-industrial year 1750 to approximately 381 parts per million today). If we stay on a so-called "business-as-usual" trajectory, the range of illustrative scenarios from the IPCC show concentrations rising anywhere from 90 percent to 250 percent over that same benchmark pre-industrial level (i.e., 530 to 970 parts per million) by the year 2100. Current concentrations have not been exceeded in the past 420,000 years – and likely not in the past 20 million years – and they remain on a path of rapid and continuing increase.

Scientists as Messengers

Sustaining a scientific definition of a problem in the public's mind can have maladaptive consequences. It partitions the issue into a zone where many people believe they are unqualified to come to their own conclusions. After all, most of us are not scientists. This means that we are relying on the testimonials of others, even if we recognize them to be underpinned by the scientific method, peer review, and a high degree of consensus.

Psychologists have documented how the identity and attributes of a "messenger" can be especially important in determining how an individual interprets a given piece of information. Is the source of information knowledgeable and trustworthy, the typical listener will ask? Do they share the listener's interests, or are they operating under the influence of some disguised agenda?

If the issue is a scientific one, people generally regard scientists as the most credible messengers. Yet when we asked the scientists participating in our Conference about the expectation that they and their colleagues will communicate – and do so forcefully when societal well-being is at stake on an issue like climate change – their answers are often sobering. They describe a system of career incentives and norms that are powerfully inhibiting (see more on this below). But they also lament the lack of training and experience that would enable them to communicate effectively beyond their peer group to broader society, even if their incentives did incline them to do so.

It is crucial, however, to distinguish between the idea that one should not always rely on scientists as messengers and the notion that scientific findings should not constitute the core content of a message. In fact, perceptions of scientific consensus appear to be an exceptionally important driver of public readiness to support action on climate change.

Steven Kull, Director of the Program on International Policy Attitudes (PIPA) at the University of Maryland and a participant in our Conference, found in a 2005 poll that those who believe that there is a scientific consensus are much more inclined to believe that even high-cost steps are needed to mitigate climate change. Among those who believe that scientists are divided, only 17 percent favored high-cost steps, as compared to 51 percent of those who perceive there is a consensus.

It is crucial, however, to distinguish between the idea that one should not always rely on scientists as messengers and the notion that scientific findings should not constitute the core content of a message. In fact, perceptions of scientific consensus appear to be an exceptionally important driver of public readiness to support action on climate change.

The poll also found that when the American public was asked to "suppose there were a survey of scientists that found that an overwhelming majority have concluded that global warming is occurring and poses a significant threat," the overall percentage who said they would then favor taking high-cost steps increased dramatically from 34 percent to 56 percent. Accordingly, the "bridging institution" called for in Recommendation #1 is specifically tasked with conducting surveys of scientists, among many other functions.

Science as a Land of Contrarians and Reversals

There are a few complications with this proposal to survey scientists or to rely on new efforts to crystallize and publicize scientific consensus more generally.

First, there have already been many group statements by distinguished scientists expressing concern about climate change and urging action, as well as one of the largest undertakings of joint science ever conducted (i.e., the Intergovernmental Panel on Climate Change). We need to better understand the reasons for their apparently limited impact. Perhaps the public believes that such declarations and peer-reviewed processes are subject to self-selection and politicization. If so, a comprehensive survey of all those scientists qualified to pass judgment, publicized as such, could be significantly more influential than these previous efforts. Or perhaps such statements and IPCC reports are indeed convincing to those who are exposed to them, but they have simply not been disseminated effectively enough to penetrate public awareness. We need more textured surveys of the public (not just the scientists) to better answer these questions, and there are social scientists ready to step up to this task.

A second caution is warranted before undertaking to measure and advertise scientific consensus. This is that few messages in our society go unanswered. One experienced social marketer at the Conference noted that, in past communications efforts where she had made a special effort to exhibit a robust scientific consensus as the centerpiece of a communications campaign, it almost instantaneously drew out those few scientists who disagreed – and with a ferocity that may have nullified the persuasive benefits of the consensus itself.

This may stem, in no small part, from the scientific temperament as well as scientific norms and methods. Science does not advance through affirmative proofs, but rather through the formulation and attempted falsification of null hypotheses that progressively whittle away alternative explanations to the one being advanced. This requires of its practitioners a contrarian stance, and many of them apply this to proclamations of consensus. One prominent scientist at our Conference noted that scientists are "skeptical to a fault." Whether skepticism is a fault or an indispensable engine of scientific progress is a legitimate question, but the point here is that it can complicate efforts to translate science into societal action. Scientists have a strong predilection to emphasize puzzles, uncertainties, caveats and details rather than to repeat core points of any consensus, even one they believe in.

A third challenge to the survey plan is that science, for all its authoritativeness, appears to many Americans to be a realm of perpetual discovery and reversals. Despite the indication in Kull's poll that the public is highly susceptible to persuasion by scientific consensus, Americans also perceive science as a contentious enterprise in which the prevailing consensus has often been overturned – often by heroic iconoclasts whose claim to fame is that they resisted conforming to what later became regarded as a laughably misguided consensus. It is no coincidence that Michael Crichton, a best-selling author with a genius for appealing to the American psyche, reportedly modeled his sympathetic scientist in the misleading novel *State of Fear* on one of the few skeptics still dissenting from the consensus view that climate change is a problem. But we're surrounded by non-fiction examples too, all the way back to grade school. Copernicus cautiously overturned Ptolemy's theory that the Earth was the center of the universe, which had dominated European astronomy for 1000 years. And Galileo famously lost his freedom for defending Copernicus' revolutionary idea, before recanting to avoid execution. Dietary science would appear to provide Americans with regular exposure to science's erratic nature: chocolate and red wine were bad for you, now they're good for you, etc. The food pyramid long inflicted on us has now been rebuilt. And so it goes.

Watching these debates and reversals from outside – without the benefit of seeing the excruciatingly careful methods underlying the best science – the average American can perhaps be excused for taking a wait-and-see approach while the experts debate their way to resolution. This perception requires that scientists do a better job of explaining the changes and updates in their understanding, which are often more nuanced than the stark reversal perceived by the public.

The "Coming Ice Age" as a Famous "Reversal" of Science

In the case of climate change, a good place to start would be to explain much more clearly, and repetitively, to the public and decision-makers alike the real story behind the ice age "scare" of the mid-1970s. That single episode during the maturation of the atmospheric sciences has served as a mainstay of editorialists and skeptics sowing confusion about the state of climate change science today, and has not been effectively put into context.

The somewhat oversimplified explanation is that three key drivers of climate change were coming into better focus in the mid-1970s, but scientists had yet to understand their relative strength: 1) ice age cycles caused by slow variations in the Earth's orbit; 2) the reflective, cooling effects of sulfate aerosols from man-made air pollution; and 3) the heat-trapping effects of increased greenhouse gas concentrations, also from human sources. Some scientists indeed produced a faulty projection of the net effect of these three, seeing the cooling from sulfate aerosols as predominant and speculating that continuation of such a trend could tip the climate toward an accelerated cooling or even an ice age. The multi-decade period of northern hemispheric cooling then prevailing (which ended in 1976) was also apparently a factor behind these inferences.

Yet the scientific consensus at the time was responsibly cautious, a fact that seems to have since been lost to the public amidst the popularization of the dramatic ice age scenario. In 1975, for example, the U.S. National Academy of Sciences (NAS) and the National Research Council issued a report called *Understanding Climate Change: A Program for Action*, which said: ". . . we do not have a good quantitative understanding of our climate machine and what determines its course. Without this fundamental understanding, it does not seem possible to predict climate. . . ." Climate modeling was still in its infancy and the report essentially called for more research, given growing recognition of the history of climatic instability and its impacts.

By 1979, however, the scientific case was firming up that warming would likely predominate over cooling if carbon dioxide emissions continued to increase, as evidenced by a National Academy of Sciences study led by Massachusetts Institute of Technology scientist Jule Charney (see "Carbon Dioxide and Climate," Washington, D.C.: National Academy of Sciences, 1979).

This brief account indicates the measured caution with which concern about climate change actually emerged, and varies considerably from the picture Americans might otherwise have of indecisive scientists flitting impetuously from one doomsday scenario to another.

Yet it is unrealistic to think that complex explanations like this – describing an evolving scientific understanding of the net effect of competing forces – can be propagated easily through the channels of our sound bite-oriented media today. And the news media are, like it or not, the primary source of most Americans' environmental education. A Yale Environmental Poll in 2005, for example, found that television news programs were the most frequently mentioned source for environmental information, with 67 percent of Americans citing them.

Here is where the Conference's educationally oriented recommendations come into play, in an effort to provide venues for contextual knowledge and understanding. One recommendation calls for incorporating climate change content into K-12 curricula (Recommendation #28). While there is a great deal of core material on climate change that could be covered, one could envision the "ice age" episode being thoughtfully treated in this context. It might fit not only in a science course module, but also in a history of science module in a social studies curriculum. Such material should, if the instructional design is sound, generate a better student grasp of how science is conducted and corrected – and how it can mature to a point where the findings really do become a compelling basis for action, a threshold that many believe we are well past on climate change today.

Another recommendation urges the strengthening of citizen-science initiatives specifically on climate change, so that Americans can get hands-on experience participating in scientific endeavors and thereby gain greater insight into how science develops (Recommendation #4). From Audubon's Christmas bird counts that have indicated the changing northerly latitudes of bird migrations to the contribution by thousands of citizens of their idle desktop computer time to major climate modeling projects administered by ClimatePrediction.net, citizen-science is an intriguing and so far under-exploited avenue for engaging Americans on the climate change issue.

Science Loves the Written Word, but Society Loves TV and Video Games

Scientists prefer the written word, whereas climate change needs to be portrayed more visually if it is going to resonate with a society increasingly gravitating away from the written word to the various visual media, whether TV imagery, animation, web games or other vehicles. A key image in this mix, at least on TV, needs to be human faces.

Communications about climate change very rarely feature human faces, and the cumulative impact of this void has been to reinforce the idea that the issue somehow has implications for polar bears and ice sheets – but not for people!

Out at the cutting-edge, the emerging field of immersive, virtual reality has been under-leveraged to date in its capacity to vividly and experientially communicate the implications of climate change.

Communications about climate change very rarely feature human faces, and the cumulative impact of this void has been to reinforce the idea that the issue somehow has implications for polar bears and ice sheets – but not for people!

Recommendation #30 calls for incorporating climate change content into instructional technologies, broadly construed to include not just educational simulations like SimCity™, but also video games and other entertainment formats more likely to reach and engage the youth segment. Making climate change fun and engaging may not seem easy at first blush, until one sees what SimCity™ did for metropolitan planning.

Google Earth, for example, is a tool that could be augmented with climate change content. Launched in June 2005, this application has rapidly popularized Internet-based "virtual globes" by bringing them to the non-expert's desktop (NASA's World Wind is another). Such innovations should be harnessed to create new opportunities for the public to visualize the effects of climate change in their locality and the planet as a whole – and, as Google Earth so elegantly permits, to zoom in and out between the two, reinforcing our dependence on the larger planetary system. Rita Colwell, former head of the National Science Foundation, was quoted in the journal *Nature* describing geographical information systems (the professional antecedents of Internet tools like Google Earth) as "the ultimate, original, multidisciplinary language" (*Nature* 439, 16 February 2006: 763). Given the language obstacles to public understanding of scientific discourse on climate change discussed earlier, these image-driven approaches hold out new potential for communicating not just across scientific disciplines, but also from scientists to non-scientists.

As described in *Nature*, Google Earth and its counterparts go far beyond a communication tool. They combine a set of rapidly advancing technologies (geographical information systems, remote-sensing, data-mining and global positioning systems) that enable the collection and integration of location-specific information. These offer the possibility of changing and profoundly democratizing the conduct of science. Consistent with Conference Recommendation #3, volunteer citizen-scientists could be recruited to submit data that would be rapidly aggregated with the inputs of others and visualized into a full picture. These advances in spatial data representation, moreover, are useful to the scientists themselves; many are, as reported in *Nature,* increasingly using Google Earth to overlay multiple data sets, and to thereby visualize complex systems (including weather) as an aid to hypothesis formulation.

Finally, we have considered words and pictures, but what about sounds? We know that many people are auditory learners. We know that many Americans believe – to this day – that they helped to cut global warming risk starting back in the 1970s by giving up their aerosol spray cans (many Americans confuse the ozone protection and climate change issues, and in fact CFC propellants are culprits in both, though decades ago the phase-out was driven by the ozone issue alone).

But one might ask why the environmentally negative impacts of aerosol spray cans stick so vividly in people's memory, whereas greenhouse gas emissions out of car tailpipes don't? Here's a simplistic, and certainly debatable, hypothesis: maybe it's that hissing sound. Aerosol spray cans sound like a damaging gas, and indeed they were. Greenhouse gases, by contrast, are not only invisible, but silent.

What if we experimented by putting a hissing device on each tailpipe? What if the thermostat hissed when you turned it up on a winter day? These are implausible options, but they reinforce a point: we need to think freshly about what people pay attention to, what drives them to make connections (bad sounds = bad environmental effects), what they retain in memory – and ultimately, what drives behavior.

FROM SCIENCE TO VALUES

Given the challenges with propagating the science of climate change throughout society, many people now favor shifting to a values-based approach to motivating action on the issue. Religious communities, in particular, are increasingly adopting the climate change issue in fulfillment of their stewardship values. Yet a science-to-values repositioning, whether religious or secular, carries risks of its own that need to be understood and managed.

Many contend that science can only take us so far. At some point – and a number of our Conference participants believe we are now there on climate change – values must be invoked and the normative impulse must come to the fore.

Indeed, a number of religious communities and ecumenical initiatives have in recent years developed an emerging moral and spiritual outline of the climate change issue. Yet this impulse is now expanding: political, business, scientific and other leaders increasingly acknowledge the limits of standard rational discourse in portraying the risks and obligations associated with climate change and find themselves digging more deeply to find an authentic, values-based foundation for responding.

Educators at our Conference, for example, said that climate change must move beyond the science classroom and into the arts, humanities, and social sciences, where issues of human values, choices and tradeoffs are more actively discussed and engaged. Some of our participating politicians advised that only a moral appeal will break through the legislative torpor on climate change. Cognitive linguists told us that climate change must be connected to deeply-framed identities and values that condition how all issues – scientific or otherwise – are interpreted.

This is most apparent in the increasing view that religious communities in America, especially the fast-growing evangelical movement, may be the single most pivotal force in the U.S. for prompting societal action on climate change.

Religious Values and Climate Change

Connecting climate change to religious values, pivotal though it may be, faces significant remaining obstacles. Our Conference recognized the centuries-long break between religion and science, which persists to this day in religious suspicion of the scientific framing of climate change and other issues. Scientists are not always seen as credible messengers by religious groups, in part because they are often perceived to favor a meaningless, purposeless and Godless world that is anathema to religious people. The evolution/creationism debate, in particular, has continued to fuel religious distrust of scientists.

Related to the religious-science divide is the pronounced religious suspicion of environmentalists. Climate change has largely been framed as an environmental crisis instead of a moral or spiritual crisis, whereas religious constituencies are motivated especially by spiritual and social justice appeals. Many religious groups perceive that environmentalists are less concerned about human beings, including the risks of job loss. Accordingly, some religious leaders – though concerned with the environment – have avoided partnerships with environmentalists and instead fashioned their own distinctive approach and vocabulary, as in *Creation Care* magazine, which is produced by the Evangelical Environmental Network.

This is most apparent in the increasing view that religious communities in America, especially the fast-growing evangelical movement, may be the single most pivotal force in the U.S. for prompting societal action on climate change.

The religious leaders at our Conference, and others who engaged with them on what they believe is needed from religious communities, produced a set of compelling recommendations that could go a long way toward promoting societal action on climate change. The recommendations called on religious leaders and communities "to recognize the scale, urgency and moral dimension of climate change, and the ethical unacceptability of any action that damages the quality and viability of life on Earth, particularly for the poor and most vulnerable" (Recommendation #11). But more than this, other recommendations explicitly called on the leaders to communicate this concern, once recognized, to their memberships (Recommendation #13) and to the nation's political leadership and broader public (Recommendation #14).

Religious communities have been at this awhile, of course – educating their memberships, issuing compelling public statements of concern, buying renewable energy from organizations like Interfaith Power & Light, and other activities.

But there does appear to have been a recent acceleration in activity. For example, in February 2006, 86 evangelical Christian leaders issued a manifesto entitled "Climate Change: An Evangelical Call for Action," encouraging the education of Christians about climate change and urging the U.S. Congress to enact legislation establishing a market-based cap-and-trade system. The manifesto appeared to significantly elevate climate change on the evangelical agenda when it said:

> "With the same love of God and neighbor that compels us to preach salvation through Jesus Christ, protect unborn life, preserve the family and the sanctity of marriage, defend religious freedom and human dignity, and take the whole gospel to a hurting world, we the undersigned evangelical leaders resolve to come together with others of like mind to pray and to work to stop global warming."

Yet despite this strong statement, the evangelical community remains divided. Days before the release of the manifesto, 22 conservative evangelical Christian leaders, including particularly prominent ones like James Dobson, founder of Focus on the Family, Charles Colson, founder of Prison Fellowship Ministries, and Richard Land, President of the Ethics and Religious Liberty Commission of the Southern Baptist Convention, wrote to their umbrella group, the National Association of Evangelicals (NAE), asking that its leadership refrain from signing the statement – an appeal that succeeded. Their stated rationale was that "Global warming is not a consensus issue. . . ." Some of the dissenters noted that, by comparison, the poverty issue was not as controversial and that action on climate change could undermine their anti-poverty agenda by diverting dollars needed to lift the poor.

Although they did not cite it, the dissenting evangelicals' position bears similarities to the ranking exercise conducted by the Copenhagen Consensus initiative, which put a high priority on investing in immediate poverty alleviation (malnutrition, disease, sanitation) over allegedly distant, and economically discounted, threats like climate change. Anecdotally, leaders of foundations have also privately described the moral difficulty of navigating this tradeoff as they make funding decisions. While they might recognize the seriousness of climate change and the importance of funding a successful strategy, the same dollar could be spent directly on pills to save African children from river blindness – a relatively more concrete, quantifiable outcome. This suggests that more work needs to be done to clarify the exacerbating impact of climate change on poverty, on one hand, and to advance a coordinated basis for setting and measuring concrete progress in addressing climate change so that it can compete for a place on the agenda.

At the Conference, religious evangelicals spoke as well about obstacles that relate back to our earlier discussion of whether communications about the threatening consequences of climate change are less likely to motivate a societal response than positive messages. Some contended that the formulation of climate change as an issue requiring sacrifice and changes in lifestyles has undermined its ability to break through to certain religious communities.

Evangelicals, in particular, are often repelled by gloom-and-doom messages on matters like population control, which imply a need for big government. They noted at the Conference that this resistance might be overcome if the climate change issue were reframed as an opportunity to live a more morally and spiritually fulfilling life.

Given such obstacles, it is not reasonable to assume that all religious leaders and communities will readily respond to the Conference recommendation that they recognize the moral dimension of climate change or that they should establish religion-science and religion-environmentalist partnerships across longstanding lines of distrust (Recommendation #19). Some have succeeded in blazing this path – see, for example, the National Religious Partnership for the Environment's 2004 statement "Earth's Climate Embraces Us All," which was co-signed by religious and scientific leaders (*www.nrpe.org/issues/i_air/air_interfaith01.htm*).

Evangelicals, in particular, are often repelled by gloom-and-doom messages on matters like population control, which imply a need for big government. They noted at the Conference that this resistance might be overcome if the climate change issue were reframed as an opportunity to live a more morally and spiritually fulfilling life.

Such cross-domain statements and partnerships should be created or expanded where and when all sides are ready. But some at our Conference noted that doing so prematurely may cause the taint associated with environmentalism to slow down the nascent religious impulse to adopt the climate change issue. In such cases, it may make sense to start with exploratory dialogues across these domains on a discreet, low-profile basis.

The eminent Harvard University biologist E.O. Wilson writes of having attended such a dialogue – a two-day retreat of the U.S. Roman Catholic Bishops to discuss the relation of science to religion. He notes that one professor of theology said there: "Science went out the door with Aquinas and we never invited her back" (Edward O. Wilson, *The Future of Life*, Alfred A. Knopf, 2002: 159). But after days of vigorous discussion, one of their highest priorities for post-conference study was environment and conservation. Indeed such study and research can help pave the way for cross-domain partnerships to develop and thrive, and accordingly, Conference Recommendation #17 calls for further expanding the scholarly field of Religion and Ecology so as to create a deeper base of mutual knowledge to supply nascent dialogues and understandings.

Politicians and Values

Values are often cited in the political arena as an explanation for divisions between people – divisions that are, if not irreconcilable, at least inhibiting to convergent or bipartisan action. We will discuss the issue of partisanship and climate change more below. Here we note simply that a significant theme at our Conference was that liberals and conservatives are motivated by distinct and deeply rooted sets of values, which influence their political preferences on climate change and a range of other issues.

Others contend, however, that appeals to common values provide a promising avenue for overcoming differences and engendering societal action on issues like climate change. An example cited at the Conference was former President Ronald Reagan, who won two terms despite documented gaps between his positions and the public's majority preferences on key issues. His success, therefore, was attributed to his ability to talk about issues as a door into a deeper discussion of values, where he was more closely aligned with the American public.

In this view, values are the key driver of the public's decision-making and until those favoring action on climate change do a better job of connecting the issue to values – not just religious values, but lifestyle values like hunting, which may be threatened by climate change – they will not advance the issue.

A key recommendation of the Politics working group at our Conference, therefore, is to "recast climate change as a moral and faith issue, not a scientific or environmental one" and to "catalyze a broader coalition of allies around this moral common ground" (Recommendation #21).

Authentic Messengers

One way to produce societal action on the basis of mainstream values may be to find mainstream voices prepared to speak out on climate change – farmers, hunters, fishermen, rank-and-file labor union members, local TV meteorologists, soccer moms, NASCAR drivers, and moderate politicians, among others. Recruitment must be based on a genuine process of engagement, however, not an effort to find and script puppets. This is important for ethical reasons. But is also strategically sound: people have been shown, in laboratory experiments, and in real life, to be adept at detecting when they are being manipulated, even subtly. They discount scripted events or speakers and the reliability of the information being conveyed. So a key need is to find *authentic* messengers on climate change, those who can speak convincingly and honestly about the issue from their own perspective, outside the orchestration of a modern issue campaign.

Finding and cultivating authentic messengers will require introducing prospects to information and perhaps values associated with climate change, and permitting them to find their own voice on the issue, rather than imposing a didactic model on the exchange. BP, for example, has aired an effective series of "person on the street" television advertisements in which average citizens (reportedly not scripted actors) verbalize their own concerns about the implications of society's – and their own – energy use, including in relation to climate change. Putting aside any debates about BP's motives, the advertisements struck a chord because of their authenticity: the citizens describe their uncertainties, dilemmas, and concerns openly. Communicators working on the issue of climate change may be able to take a page out of the BP book by taking more time to listen to citizens' concerns about being asked to take action on climate change – what tradeoffs do they fear, what impingements on their quality of life, what uncertainties would they like to resolve?

A recurring theme at the Conference was that the most persuasive and trusted channel for propagating information on controversial issues like climate change is peer-to-peer dialogue. News editors may listen to esteemed fellow news editors who say they're missing the biggest story of our time by not covering climate change – hence the call for orchestrating editor-to-editor dialogues (Recommendation #7). Religious congregations may listen to their fellow parishioners speaking about the spiritual imperatives associated with climate change (Recommendation #13).

Many concerned with advancing climate change messages believe that novel voices must be recruited and deployed in order to jolt people awake and prompt them to take a fresh look at the issue. On the surface, this point is distinct from the call for authentic voices. And yet, look again. One way to read this is that novelty can be a surrogate for authenticity. It is precisely when a speaker deviates from a predictable script that we are compelled to take notice, in part because it forces us to at least consider that the person is speaking authentically from the heart. This may, in turn, induce people to take a closer look at the issue they're talking about.

Observe Caution in Moving from Science to Values

Despite all the recommendations in its favor, we should observe caution in moving too quickly from science-based communications to moral and values-based appeals, recognizing not only the benefits but the risks of doing so.

> ➤ First, while many values are socially constructed, some are personal and may not allow for the level of commonality needed to achieve a societal consensus for action. Even social values often emerge in an oppositional sense, whether in conscious or unconscious distinction to the values of others.

> ➤ Second, values are subjective – by definition, they do not lend themselves to objective verification. Thus a prominent elected official at the Conference cautioned against the recommendation to recast climate change from a scientific to a moral issue, because he believes that the scientific rigor associated with climate change science, once recognized more fully than it is today, can serve as an objective basis for eventual convergence among officials from different parties.

> ➤ Third, people tend to apply extra scrutiny to individuals whose assertions are made using the language of values. In this sense, values may be less susceptible to influence from outside than is recognized. The pathway to influence through "information" that is less value-laden may be comparatively more open.

One might counter that the recommendations call less for changing values per se, than for tapping into deeply rooted values *already held* by the person one is seeking to influence. That may be valid in theory, but the distinction in practice can be hard to draw. If you are seeking to tell someone what the implications of their values are, you are in well-defended terrain and the obstacles to your success may be higher, as they should be. Yet the gains, if successful, may be greater – and more enduring.

What can be gained, by contrast, through an information-based approach, rather than a values approach? An anecdote from the Conference is telling, though certainly not conclusive. One of the participating religious leaders said he had come to embrace climate change as a spiritually crucial issue, but had done so by being exposed to the science and undergoing something akin to a "conversion experience." In other words, it was the science, not the values per se, that were most persuasive to him, which only then led to his spiritual interpretation of the issue.

It turns out that the person who exposed him to the science and prompted the epiphany was a religious scientist, so we cannot in this particular case cleanly distinguish the scientific from the religious influences. Yet it's clear that the science was an important ingredient in the persuasive mix. This leaves us with the insight that we may not need to frame science and values as mutually exclusive alternatives, but rather as considerations that can work in tandem. This anecdote also implies the value of recruiting more such dual-identity individuals to build these bridges in our society: religious scientists, politician-scientists, journalist-scientists, religious politicians and other permutations. We had several such rare individuals at our Conference and they provided crucial connective tissue.

One of the participating religious leaders at the Conference said he had come to embrace climate change as a spiritually crucial issue, but had done so by being exposed to the science and undergoing something akin to a "conversion experience." In other words, it was the science, not the values per se, that were most persuasive to him, which only then led to his spiritual interpretation of the issue.

Tradeoffs

Meaningful discussions about values are usually about tradeoffs, not stand-alone commitments. It is one thing for someone to agree that climate change is a serious problem, or even to say their values call on them to do something about it. It is quite another for them to give climate change a privileged place in a forced ranking of values – or to demonstrate behaviorally that they are willing to sacrifice something for it, including through a demonstrated "willingness to pay."

This was evidenced earlier in our discussion of the perceived climate/poverty tension. Putting aside potentially overlooked evidence of the linkages between the two issues, they are frequently perceived as requiring hard tradeoffs (and they do, in relation to intergenerational implications). This and other value tradeoffs complicate the application of values to action in the case of climate change. Economists bring their arsenal of quantification tools in an attempt to reconcile these as much as possible into one integrated account, but the most intellectually honest among them concede the limits of their method in quantifying non-marketed goods and intangibles, and in accounting for potentially irreversible issues like climate change.

One religious leader at the Conference noted that business leaders are much more credible messengers to his parishioners about climate change than environmentalists.

Political scientist Arthur Lupia, a participant at our Conference, has done celebrated research that relates to this issue of value tradeoffs. He conducted experiments to ascertain what causes a messenger to be perceived as credible. In simplest terms, the answer is that speakers perceived as both knowledgeable and trustworthy are the most credible. Trustworthiness, however, is not simply a function of character, but rather the existence of institutional or other contextual penalties imposed on an untruthful speaker. Listeners are sensitive to the conditions under which speech is uttered, not just the content. If the speaker is perceived as facing adverse and probable consequences from lying (i.e., a tradeoff), then the listener is more likely to give credence to what they say. (See Arthur Lupia and Mathew D. McCubbins, *The Democratic Dilemma: Can Citizens Learn What They Need to Know?* Cambridge University Press, 1998.)

This finding was exhibited at our Conference in the following way: One religious leader noted that business leaders are much more credible messengers to his parishioners about climate change than environmentalists. Whereas environmentalists are often perceived as oblivious to the tradeoffs by which climate change policies may produce job losses in some sectors, business leaders are seen to be clearly measuring their position on climate change in relation to exactly this job loss risk. In other words, the business leader's expression of concern about climate change carries real costs and is therefore more credible.

Building on this insight, Recommendation #15 calls for new dialogues on climate change between business and religious leaders and their respective constituencies.

PACKAGING CLIMATE CHANGE AS AN ENERGY ISSUE

Frustrated by the inability of climate change to break through as an urgent public concern, many believe it is best to finally admit that the issue cannot stand on its own. Climate change can be packaged with other issues that have generated more public concern to date – and energy security is a leading candidate. This is a promising strategy, but it also risks deemphasizing climate change mitigation as an explicit societal priority precisely when it needs to move up on the list.

So far we have discussed the challenges and opportunities of communicating the science of climate change and doing more to connect the issue with the core values, especially religious values, of Americans.

Some at our Conference contended, however, that there is a more compelling, if indirect, path to promoting societal action on climate change. In this view, climate change has not been conceptualized or communicated enough to the general public, and even to many leaders, as fundamentally an issue of energy. As a result, it has been fraught with more baggage and complexity than necessary. Some even noted that a campaign jingle like: "It's the energy, stupid" could help crystallize this connection.

If energy is recognized as the linchpin, it becomes possible to reframe the climate change debate as one about profit-making opportunities (for many but not all sectors) and interconnections with other valued goals like energy independence, jobs, national security and even local air quality. Indeed, the Iraq war, persistently high gas prices, and a growing awareness of the geopolitical risks associated with importing over 50 percent of our oil, mostly from volatile regions of the world, have produced a bipartisan energy independence bandwagon that climate change could jump onto. A 2005 Yale Environmental Poll showed that 92 percent of Americans see our dependence on foreign oil as a serious national problem, whereas only 66 percent regard climate change that way.

Accordingly, key leaders at our Conference crafted a summary statement that garnered broad enthusiasm among the participants though, as with all the recommendations, not formal sign-off (see box, next page).

> ## A Transformative National Effort on Energy
>
> The 2005 Yale F&ES Conference on Climate Change recognized that there is an urgent need and a compelling opportunity for a transformative national effort on energy. The rapidly changing demands of climate stabilization, international competitiveness, national security, and global poverty underscore the need for urgent national action.
>
> The energy transformation presents a significant business opportunity for almost every sector of the national economy, including: transportation, fuels, consumer goods and the agricultural community; flexible fueled vehicles and a renewed auto manufacturing sector; a modernized national grid system, linking utilities in a more secure network; an aggressive national conservation effort, based on excellent initiatives already started at the state and local level; an initiative on green buildings; and a major national effort to explore new and far-reaching energy generation activities.
>
> The achievement of the needed transformation will be greatly assisted by clarification by our national leadership of the policies needed for working in a carbon-constrained environment (e.g., market-based mechanisms); engaging the business and financial sectors in accelerating reporting related to their "carbon footprint;" encouraging the insurance industry to augment efforts to understand and communicate risk related to climate change; and encouraging the United States to begin negotiations with the global community on next steps under the U.N. Framework Convention on Climate Change.

Conference Recommendations #20 and #34 translated key elements of this vision into a proposed action. Recommendation #20 reads:

> "Design and execute a 'New Vision for Energy' campaign to encourage a national market-based transition to alternative energy sources. Harness multiple messages tailored to different audiences that embed the climate change issue in a larger set of co-benefit narratives, such as:
>
> • reducing U.S. dependency on Middle East oil (national security);

- penetrating global export markets with American innovations (U.S. stature);

- boosting U.S. job growth (jobs);

- cutting local air pollution (health)."

A number of important private initiatives have been launched to address the complex issues associated with American energy use, such as the Energy Future Coalition, Set America Free, Securing America's Future Energy (SAFE), the Apollo Alliance, and the National Commission on Energy Policy. They have drawn news media and public attention for their breadth of support, including what are widely regarded as unlikely suspects and unusual bedfellows – showing that this has increasingly become a fertile arena for cross-domain collaboration.

The initiatives are sector-specific and in many cases highly detailed in their prescriptions for action. The Energy Future Coalition, for example, has helped to forge a promising initiative called "25 x 25", which holds out a compelling vision that: "Agriculture will provide 25 percent of the total energy consumed in the United States by 2025 while continuing to produce abundant, safe and affordable food and fiber." The initiative is being led by crop, livestock and tree farmers, as well as horticulturalists, and energy and policy specialists. Their primary focus is on accelerating the scale-up of biofuels production, such as ethanol and biodiesel from dedicated energy crops as well as agricultural waste residues. But their plan extends to generating energy from wind and solar installations on farms, as well as from methane gas emissions from agricultural operations.

Given the existence of so many worthwhile initiatives, it is worth asking whether a new one, as called for by the Conference, is necessary or not. Answering that requires a fuller assessment of the extent to which current initiatives are succeeding – and if so, according to what metric? Do they need to be improved? Would they perform better in fulfilling their objectives if they were more closely coordinated with one another – or even combined? Or is it better to have different initiatives mobilizing different constituencies with somewhat distinct emphases in their messages and prescriptions? Under any of these scenarios, how can we best ensure that climate change is heavily weighted in their prescriptions, actions and communications? These are crucial questions that those of us carrying the Conference recommendations forward must answer.

The Risks of Issue Packaging – Manageable But Not Trivial

There are clearly benefits to strategically packaging the climate change issue with energy security and other co-benefits. At the same time, there are a handful of cautions to observe:

> First, there is no guarantee that steps taken to reduce oil imports will also mitigate climate change. Energy efficiency investments often will. But certain energy supply choices may not. For example, a race is now on to accelerate the exploitation of U.S. coal reserves and northern Alberta tar sands. Both will reduce our dependence on oil imports from unstable regions of the world, and yet they will exacerbate climate change – unless costly ancillary steps to capture and sequester carbon emissions are also taken. This is an inherent risk in any agenda that lists climate change as an objective, but a subsidiary one – many of the existing bipartisan energy initiatives referenced above list climate change in the third or fourth slot of priorities, if at all. If climate change science is not in the driver's seat as far as calibrating the speed and level of our future emissions reductions, we run a significant risk that packaged prescriptions will be inadequate.

> Second, energy issues are high on the public agenda today but could subside, as they have in the past. This seems unlikely, given signs of heightening geopolitical risks and evidence that oil prices have ascended to a new and higher equilibrium. But if cheap energy should come again, or we are able to pull American troops back from the Middle East, energy could become less of a preoccupation, taking climate change down with it as part of that package. Moreover, it is exactly when energy prices fall that energy overuse becomes more likely, further exacerbating climate change.

> Third, subsuming an issue like climate change in a larger narrative means that one inevitably sacrifices some amount of awareness-building on the climate issue itself. To the extent that such awareness would otherwise grow cumulatively through time, it is costly to interrupt that natural process of issue maturation and growth in societal understanding. At a very basic level, doesn't a problem need to be well understood, and explicitly so, to be solved?

> Fourth, climate change is a multi-faceted issue whose causes and consequences can be portrayed from a variety of angles and in

relation to many constituencies. This makes it amenable to audience segmentation and messaging flexibility in a narrowcasting world (e.g., pitch farmers on the agricultural biofuels part of the greenhouse gas reduction equation). Yet this very plurality can be the enemy of public understanding: if an issue comes to mean many things to many people, how can the distracted citizen or legislator keep track of it, wrap their mind around it, and propose to do something about it? This is where goal-setting becomes important. If the goal is to create a portfolio of sector-specific strategies to address climate change, then this kind of segmented approach makes great sense. If, on the other hand, one is seeking a concerted national strategy – such as a stringent cap-and-trade regulation – a greater level of strategic and messaging coordination is required. This is not to say that different constituencies cannot have different reasons for supporting a common policy – they almost always do. But it does suggest that those managing the packaging exercise described in this Conference recommendation must be cognizant of this need for a cumulative and reinforcing focus on climate change among otherwise disparate initiatives.

➤ Fifth, some contend that it is simply premature and risky to concede defeat on communicating the climate change issue on its own terms, since we have not yet applied our best talents to the task. We have not yet assembled the best data we can on how public attitudes form, change and persist on climate change (see Conference Recommendations #25 and #26 about the need to leverage the social sciences). We have not yet tapped the enormous marketing and creative talents in America on behalf of this high-stakes issue. Given this, the climate change issue should not be packaged with others lightly or out of a sense of resignation, but only after determining that the benefits of doing so outweigh the negatives. The various energy initiatives discussed above should, and will, go forth. The distinct question we are considering here is the extent to which those pursuing societal action on climate change should join forces with and devote resources to the energy independence bandwagon, versus sustaining parallel efforts more explicitly focused on climate change per se.

INCENTIVES

> *It is tempting to reduce the challenge of promoting action on climate change to matters of communications and strategic positioning. Yet this will usually only take us part of the way. Translating awareness into action depends on identifying – and selectively modifying – the deeper incentive structures at play in our society. Harnessing climate change objectives to the material incentives to modify energy supply and use patterns is an important part of the equation. But a more thorough domain-by-domain analysis of career and organizational incentives yields additional levers for fashioning a broad-based set of strategies.*

We found value at the Conference in digging below the communications layer to the stratum where incentives shape behavior. We did not limit this to career incentives, though that became a focus given the professional identities associated with most of our eight working groups. Career has become arguably the most identity-defining feature of life in modern democratic capitalism, and career incentives almost universally argue against investing time in the climate change issue – whether understanding it, communicating it, or doing something about it. Climate change is not in most people's job description. That's both an obvious problem and a vastly underestimated one. In modern America, job demands have grown to be all-consuming. One takes a big risk in freelancing beyond their bounds and losing focus on who is paying you and for what. Employers hire for focus and reward focus.

Part II of this report discusses the incentives in each domain in some depth, so here only highlights and commentary are provided. The conversation about incentives is one that could usefully be broadened – to others in the same domains and beyond them to other domains that were not represented at our Conference.

Such discussions – of how incentives have impeded action to date – need not devolve into a negative exercise in hand-wringing. If conducted with candor and diligence, the insights obtained can profoundly shape the depth of the subsequent search for solutions.

Incentives often seem implacable, by their very nature. Some are so interwoven into the fabric of our society that it is almost impossible to imagine altering them. Many participants at the Conference were ready to diagnose their own incentive structures, but then recognized the long odds against changing them and preferred to focus on other, more feasible next steps.

Even where incentives appear changeable, one can be forgiven for asking whether, given the urgency of the climate change issue, resources would be better invested in more tangible, near-term activities – like communications campaigns. By the time one succeeds in modifying incentives in something as slow-changing as the university system, for example, won't it be too late to keep greenhouse gas concentrations at an acceptable level? (What level is that? See the discussion of goal-setting below.)

And yet it is worth remembering that not all incentive structures are laws of nature (some are!), but rather are often designed and administered by human beings. Some of these human beings, therefore, may be susceptible to the entreaties of determined change-agents. This will usually be a high-level activity appropriate for change-agents already in positions of institutional power, or those best situated to influence those in power. In other cases, however, such high-level emissaries may be less important than altering information flows. The way individuals calculate a response to their incentives may be amenable to new information. This, for example, is an implied rationale for Conference Recommendation #34 calling for the business community to be afforded greater access to new information about the opportunities in low-carbon technologies.

Academic Scientists' Incentives: Specialized, Peer-Focused and Publicity-Averse

What are the incentives of academic scientists to propagate their findings throughout society? Scientists are rewarded largely for success in specialized research and for communicating what they learn to their peers. Their most striking findings trickle out to a wider audience, but the scientific community, by and large, is a rarefied, walled-off world. Peers are the source of professional esteem, of reviewers for one's journal articles, and of the kind of dialogue and collaborative insights that can be critical to research breakthroughs. Given their proximity to this incentive-rich network of colleagues, most scientists resist diverting time to communicating with the media or the public, or injecting their expertise into the policy fray on issues like climate change. Most are also sensitive to reputational risks from being seen as too eager to gain public attention, or from extending beyond the secure core of their knowledge base amidst policy crossfire.

Before presuming that these tendencies should change, it is important to recognize that many regard them as crucial to the success and credibility of objective science. This does not mean, however, that the disadvantages should not be equally acknowledged when assessing their implications for the science-action gap on an issue like climate change. The costs of not having scientists speaking out can be high indeed, given their very high relative trust ranking in society; a 2005 Yale Environmental Poll found that 83 percent of Americans trust university scientists (compared to 62 percent who trust industry scientists and 56 percent who trust their state governor, for example).

Academic incentives are, as noted earlier, tradition-bound and enormously resistant to change. While many at the Conference thought changing academia was too steep a mountain to climb, others said its role as the generator and repository of scientific knowledge on climate change justified mounting a concerted influence strategy. Accordingly, Conference Recommendation #3 calls for reaching out at senior levels in universities – including to the presidents, trustees and tenure-granting faculty – to identify high-level actions that could modify the financial and reward structures within academia most responsible for inhibiting scientists from engaging in interdisciplinary research on issues like climate change and from devoting more of their time to communicating beyond their peer group.

The key here, as with many incentive structures, is persuading those in power that they would not be unilaterally "disarming" in a broader competitive battle if they made a decision to modify the incentive structures they administer.

Is there, for example, a leading research university that is prepared to modify its tenure-granting process in a way that values the public communications exertions and impact of the up-and-coming tenure candidates? Similarly, is there one that is prepared to truly value the kind of interdisciplinary research required on climate change, instead of the traditional level of specialization required for tenure and other forms of recognition?

If a specific university, sensing the strategic import of climate change, answers either question in the affirmative, will it be sending a signal that will disadvantage those tenure candidates? In other words, if junior tenure-track faculty seek to adapt to the modified incentive structure in this forward-looking university, and nonetheless fail to gain tenure there, will they still have a chance at other institutions that have not similarly adapted their evaluative model?

Any university president, provost or university committee that unilaterally tinkers with the incentive structure that cascades down to influence behavior throughout their institution must be cautious about the potential career harms that could be done, or ultimately the risks to the institution as a whole if it populates its faculty with a breed not held in high esteem elsewhere in academia. These are complicated questions that cannot be easily answered. But they deserve to be asked, today more than ever, given the societal stakes on science-driven issues like climate change. Moreover, the deliberations, once underway, should include not just those inside academia, but those who fund academia, those who provide students and tuition to academia, governments who subsidize academia, and representatives of the broader society that is deeply affected by what transpires there.

Is there, for example, a leading research university that is prepared to modify its tenure-granting process in a way that values the public communications exertions and impact of the up-and-coming tenure candidates? Similarly, is there one that is prepared to truly value the kind of interdisciplinary research required on climate change, instead of the traditional level of specialization required for tenure and other forms of recognition?

Journalists' Incentives: Get onto the Front Page

Journalists, for their part, are unlikely to see the climate change story as their ticket to career advancement. Ambitious journalists will readily admit that they wake up in the morning aiming to get onto the front page. What gets them there? Wars, the White House, fires, abductions, scandals, malfeasance, exposure of villains, and controversy more generally. Not climate change, except in its most controversial or most politicized moments. So the most talented journalists tend to gravitate to other beats, often the political beat since it tends to breed future editors. There are, of course, exceptions – including some whose internal compass tells them that this story simply needs to be written about and others who recognize that the issue may mature to the point when it will get the prominent coverage it warrants and they'll be well-positioned to supply it by having started early.

Meanwhile, it is news editors – not the laws of nature – who determine day-in and day-out what goes on the front page (albeit constrained, over time, by market pressures from readers and advertisers). Persuading editors that climate change is an important topic worthy of recurring front-page space may well be feasible if a good case can be made, and delivered by the "messengers" most credible to them. In this spirit, the Conference recommended an initiative to foster a series of visits and conferences whereby respected journalists and editors informed on climate change can speak to their peer editors, whom the Conference participants referred to as "gatekeepers," indicating their control over many of the on-the-ground incentives operating in the news media profession (Recommendation #7).

Entreaties from top scientists associated with the proposed bridging institution (Recommendation #1) – while lacking this peer-to-peer element – could also be influential in securing more news coverage and editorial attention if they succeed in obtaining audiences with key editorial page editors, managing editors, TV producers, media owners, columnists, commentators, and anchors, and briefing them on the stakes.

Educators' Incentives: Teach to the Test

Teachers are increasingly obligated to concentrate their instruction on content that is covered by high-stakes exit exams as a result of the accountability provisions of the No Child Left Behind Act (NCLB). After an initial focus on mathematics and reading testing, which some argue has had the effect of de-emphasizing science teaching across the country, the NCLB law will require state testing on science starting in the fall of 2007. State preparation for this new accountability on science education provides a valuable window of opportunity for promoting the incorporation of climate change content.

Until this happens, it is unlikely that most teachers will divert classroom time to the teaching of climate change. Making it part of the standards-based curriculum rather than an optional topic will also mitigate the disincentive teachers face when it comes to teaching controversial topics that might provoke a parental backlash.

At present, state science standards address earth sciences but rarely blend in climate change. In some states, climate change receives parenthetical mention, but to ensure significant student exposure and understanding it needs to be woven in as a significant content or subject area. Conference Recommendation #28 could prove especially important in favorably modifying the key incentives by incorporating climate change into state science standards, and by calling for the design of the climate change curriculum and the training of teachers needed to fulfill those standards.

Politicians' Incentives: Limited Accountability on Climate Change and a Stigma to Boot

No matter how focused on the public interest they may be, the politicians' incentive structure is inescapably dominated by the need to get elected or reelected. Many political candidates, and the operatives who orchestrate their campaigns, believe that environmental issues – especially global ones like climate change – offer little opportunity to carve out electoral advantage. And polling of the public largely bears this out – only a small minority of the electorate deems the environment a voting issue (though there is some evidence the Independents in this group could constitute a swing vote in close elections). In recent presidential campaigns, nominees who had championed the environment (and climate change specifically) throughout their careers appeared to mute their support because of perceived electoral downsides.

Yet private discussions with campaign operatives reveal that some indeed perceive a stigma associated with talking about climate change on the campaign trail, which could render their candidate susceptible to ridicule or at least to being called "out of touch" with the concerns of average Americans. Against this downside, they perceived little compensating upside.

Not everyone agrees with this assessment, contending that the environment was discussed by the campaigns but not covered much by a media preoccupied with horse-race coverage and hot-button social issues.

Yet private discussions with campaign operatives reveal that some indeed perceive a stigma associated with talking about climate change on the campaign trail, which could render their candidate susceptible to ridicule or at least to being called "out of touch" with the concerns of average Americans. Against this downside, they perceived little compensating upside.

Some polling of political leaders indicates that while they personally favor action to address climate change, it has not risen to the top of their legislative agenda, in part because they are unaware of their constituents' general, though not uniformly urgent, support for action. The public, according to polling by Steven Kull, also tends to think that their elected officials are doing more about climate change than they actually are. As a result of this mutual non-awareness, politicians have simply not experienced much constituent pressure to act today on climate change. Consequently, there are relatively few incumbents championing the issue legislatively today, with a few promising exceptions now seeking to build on the non-binding "Sense of the Senate" resolution in 2005 favoring a mandatory cap-and-trade regulation to limit greenhouse gas emissions.

The Conference looked beneath the surface partisanship on climate change to the underlying structural problems that impede effective government action on this and other issues. For example, one incumbent elected official with us spotlighted how the prevalence of safe seats in the Congress limits the opportunity for issue entrepreneurship on climate change. When over 90 percent of elected members of Congress face no plausible threat to their incumbency in a future election, they are simply less inclined to have to respond to any constituent pressure that can be mobilized on climate change or any other issue, or to consider the electoral implications of their inaction.

This implies that those concerned with promoting societal action on climate change need to also understand and address gerrymandering, campaign finance reform, and other determinants of policy outcomes. Accordingly, Conference Recommendation #24 calls for convening a group of political scientists, elected officials, and campaign operatives to conduct an analysis and dialogue about the connections between problems in democratic governance in the U.S. and climate change specifically. It would be grandiose to think that this action, alone, could achieve outright change in these larger political structures, but it could add an additional rationale to large ongoing efforts to do so (e.g., campaign finance reform), while also ensuring that change agents focused on climate change craft more sophisticated strategies that reflect the full range of obvious and non-obvious forces at play.

Business and Finance Incentives: Profit and Fiduciary Responsibility

Business and financial professionals, for their part, face incentive structures that, on their surface, are remarkably clear-cut. They are measured on their profit-making success. Unless and until a particular business leader sees either a profit-generating opportunity or a probable cost or risk associated with climate change, their fiduciary responsibility will typically dictate that they ignore the issue, even if a values-based appeal has succeeded in pricking their conscience about the societal risks.

Within many business organizations, moreover, there are employees (usually in the government relations department) whose incentives are sharply defined to minimize regulatory burdens on the firm by lobbying diligently against climate change policies. So even if a smattering of executives in a corporation grows concerned about climate change, their organization's course as a whole may still proceed on auto-pilot in opposition to climate change action.

A similar type of organizational behavior can cause disconnects within trade associations. One member business may grow more receptive to climate change action, while its trade association leadership remains wedded to the least common denominator position of the most recalcitrant members. Even apart from this membership influence, trade associations face a fundamental incentive to demonstrate how their unique ability to aggregate and exert the membership's collective strength delivers a measurable return by minimizing regulatory burdens.

The business community is, of course, not monolithic. Some businesses are large emitters of greenhouse gases and determined to avoid regulation of any kind, even by funding disinformation campaigns on climate change science. Some are large emitters who have explicitly acknowledged the inevitability of regulation and are working to shape it to their advantage by seeking a predictable price-signal for carbon, equitability across sectors, and the flexibility to minimize costs (and avoid stranding their assets) through market-based emissions trading. Still others are providers of low-carbon technology and assets like renewable energy or efficiency enhancements, and see a profitable upside from climate change regulation.

So business' incentive structures, while tied to the profit-making motive at the highest level of analysis, can and do cause very different behaviors depending on how the business is situated and how it calculates risks and opportunities over various time horizons. These calculations are fundamentally driven by information inputs, and this is where the Conference identified a key target of opportunity. Simply put, participants noted that there is room to do much better in making businesses aware of the profitable opportunities associated with buying or selling low-carbon or no-carbon products and services.

Achieving this awareness requires not high-minded exhortations, but an increasingly tailored approach that begins with the realities of each business' capital budgeting and operational framework and proceeds to supply the analytic and decision-support tools needed to help them evaluate carbon mitigation technologies on a basis that is commensurable to other opportunities.

At the Conference, some touted the emissions-reducing efficiency gains immediately available to businesses at a cost-savings, and expressed puzzlement about why these have not been adopted already.

But others underscored all the variables that complicate adoption of new technologies – from first-cost obstacles and other financing gaps to a range of other intangible behavioral frictions such as the inertia that comes from comfort with using the "tried-and-true." There are, after all, many positive Net Present Value (NPV) investments that businesses knowingly do *not* make – due to limited execution capacity, competition from other, higher-NPV projects, choices about which activities are more strategic to the firm, and many other reasons.

How carbon mitigation fits into all this quickly becomes a complex picture of the kind that few business leaders have the time to sort out on the fly, especially in the face of other short-term pressures like quarterly earnings reports and near-term competitive threats. Accordingly, the Business & Finance group recommended the creation of an outside information intermediary to help businesses perform these calculations, and a set of eight principles to guide them in developing their internal capacity with respect to carbon-related risks and opportunities.

The first of these recommendations calls for the creation and funding of an R&D-type organization to undertake and disseminate credible and independent studies of the economic impacts of climate change on a sector-by-sector basis, as well as of the appropriate solutions (Recommendation #34). This would be an independent provider of reliable information free of any advocacy taint, and it would likely do not only original work but would also aggregate, vet and translate the many good studies already being done on this subject by academics and, as available, by private consulting firms. The envisioned mandate could also extend to provision of funds to overcome financing gaps impeding adoption of low carbon technologies, including grants to deploy pilot-scale technologies for testing and demonstration purposes.

As for the eight principles described in Recommendation #33, these would help business leaders reduce the enormity of the climate change issue to a manageable, if still ambitious, to-do list. The principles range from analyzing the firm's carbon profile (including facilities, products, suppliers) under multiple scenarios and in standardized reporting formats (i.e., pro forma P&Ls) to developing a company-wide plan to address the carbon risks and opportunities identified. To be actionable, the recommendation would need to be supplemented by detailed implementation guidance.

Among other benefits, adopting these eight principles would help American businesses close a growing shortfall with European businesses in understanding how to measure their potential carbon liability. American businesses have so far operated without a price on carbon emissions, while European companies (and American multinationals operating there) are now subject to carbon regulation through the European Union's Emissions Trading Scheme (the first phase of which runs from 2005-2007). But there are other increasing pressures on American companies that are starting to affect the way executives and fiduciaries interpret the climate change issue, from the risk of shareholder lawsuits to future U.S. regulation that could emerge well within the life-cycle of investments being made today. Energy price increases and volatility are already prompting a reexamination of exposures and trends in the U.S., a process that could usefully be expanded to include related factors like future carbon liabilities.

The eight-principle framework also calls for education of the CEO and board members on climate change and its implications. Some may object that this issue can be handled by a firm's risk managers or government relations department and need not rise to an executive or governance level. That will remain a valid point of debate as the principles are promoted and considered for adoption. But consistent with an overarching Conference theme, the lack of action on climate change stems partly from the fact that it has often been kept in a silo. Integrating the issue more fully at the strategic level, at least in businesses where it is potentially material, should help create a more robust private sector discourse on, and eventually response to, the climate change issue. Moreover, executives who are informed may be more likely to adopt another of the eight principles, which calls for businesses to engage externally in policy dialogue and to dissociate from scientific disinformation campaigns.

One of the most compelling and comprehensible cases for scaling up the adoption of low-carbon and no-carbon technologies by businesses across the world comes from S. Pacala and R. Socolow of the Carbon Mitigation Initiative at Princeton University. Rather than acting as enthusiasts for any particular technology, they categorize a range of proven technologies in relation to the overall reductions needed to stabilize greenhouse gas emissions in the atmosphere. Others have noted the disconnect between their somewhat cheerful admonitions that this can be done and the dauntingly heroic technological scale-up they prescribe. Nonetheless, their assertion in the journal *Science* bears quotation:

> "Humanity already possesses the fundamental scientific, technical, and industrial know-how to solve the carbon and climate problem for the next half-century. A portfolio of

technologies now exists to meet the world's energy needs over the next 50 years and limit atmospheric CO_2 to a trajectory that avoids a doubling of the pre-industrial concentration. Every element in this portfolio has passed beyond the laboratory bench and demonstration project; many are already implemented somewhere at full industrial scale . . . . It is important not to become beguiled by the possibility of revolutionary technology. Humanity can solve the carbon and climate problem in the first half of this century simply by scaling up what we already know how to do" (*Science* Vol. 305, No. 5686: 968).

Environmentalists' Incentives: Balancing Mission and Organizational Perpetuation

At the mission level, environmentalists face strong incentives to address climate change, especially if they subscribe to the notion advanced by Professor John Holdren of Harvard University that climate is the "envelope" within which all other environmental issues are contained. For example, even conservation-oriented groups that have traditionally refrained from advocacy on climate change or other issues in favor of land acquisition are increasingly recognizing that the very ecosystems and habitats they have preserved from developers are at significant risk from climate change.

Yet this hierarchical mission logic has arguably failed, so far, to harness the environmental community to a disciplined and organized response to the issue. For all the dedication that some environmental groups have shown on climate change, there is today a widespread belief that their cumulative impact has not as yet been adequate to the need. The Conference's incentive analysis helped to illuminate some of the reasons.

First, at the career level, the individuals who lead and work inside environmental organizations have increasingly taken on a professional cast, featuring technocratic skills such as legal, policy and scientific analysis. No doubt these skills generate measurable and important results and they align well with private and governmental sector career pathways, thereby allowing access to top talent. Nonetheless, some contend that political organizing skills are often missing in these organizations, along with, in the words of one Conference participant, the "moral energy" needed to mobilize a broad constituency for action on an issue like climate change. As we've discussed, climate change is especially well-suited at this strategic moment for values-based engagement, but some doubt that environmental groups have the particular talent base and culture to leverage this dimension of the issue.

Second, once these relatively high-cost and specialized skill-sets are accumulated in an organization, it is natural to seek the arena offering the most bang for the buck. This has generally meant that the major environmental groups focus on specific policy and legislative issues at the federal level. While this has often been a good, high-leverage bet in the past, the locus of activity on climate change has arguably shifted – for some years now – to state and local action.

For all the dedication that environmental groups have shown on climate change, there is today a widespread belief that their cumulative impact has not as yet been adequate to the need.

Third, environmental groups must attend to the ongoing realities of organizational perpetuation. This includes the need to build membership and raise money from donors and foundations. In undertaking these activities, environmental groups have a strong incentive to frame climate change as an environmental issue, whereas the issue's society-wide implications for human well-being could enable pursuit of a much broader constituency base than those traditionally responsive to environmental appeals. Some contend that the historical evolution of the environmental community, including the imperative to answer to its existing constituency base, renders it unable to effectively recruit and engage that broader constituency.

Moreover, there is an inescapably competitive element to the pursuit of organizational perpetuation. On one hand, the environmental community includes thousands of niche organizations that each specialize in a subset of issues, localities or even strategies (e.g., litigation versus land acquisition). If one issue is targeted by too many of these niche groups at once, then the pressures of membership and donor competition tend to provide a corrective – leading back toward specialization or toward organizational demise as the donors cull out the weaker, redundant groups.

On the other hand, the major environmental advocacy groups have arguably converged and grown more similar to one another as a natural result of organizational maturation and expansion. As a result, many of the key groups now have overlapping memberships, share the same suite of strategic capabilities, and find themselves jockeying for a competitive edge that will distinguish them.

The niche groups often assume that others are better positioned to address an issue of the scope of climate change, by virtue of their size or strategic capabilities – leading the niche groups to sustain their original focus on other issues. Some of the major groups, by contrast, have decided to expand their work on climate change, which then inclines them to focus on creating a superior and independently brandable strategy. Competition can, of course, stimulate better strategies, but it also risks internecine competition for limited donor and membership support.

Both responses, therefore, present potential problems for the quality of the overall effort. Many of the niche groups end up depriving the climate change effort of their local constituency and skills, at a time when localization is especially needed to generate public engagement. Meanwhile, the major groups compete and duplicate one another, sometimes frittering away resources on competition that could be better spent pursuing coordinated goals.

Many at our Conference, including major donors and foundation representatives, said that environmental organizations have simply not done a good enough job of working in partnership with each other on climate change – whether combining resources or crafting a common, mutually reinforcing, message on the issue.

So what can be done? These diagnoses imply a range of potential solutions from the grand to the highly pragmatic. At the grand end of the spectrum, at least one Conference participant suggested that global warming should be the animating issue behind a new environmentalism – one in which entire ecosystems are understood to be at risk, new values are infused, bigger goals set, organizational walls broken down, and entirely new levels of integration undertaken between environmental, energy and economic planning. Redefining the issue in such ways would require stepping back and forging a new vision, including of the organizational forms, skill-sets and missions of the "environmental community."

Recommendation #36 could serve as a first step in the direction of executing on such a vision, while still being practicable in the very short term. It calls for the formation of a Leadership Council composed of senior representatives from a variety of segments of society (business, labor, academia, government, the NGO sector, medicine, law, public health, and community leaders) that would "serve as an integrating mechanism for developing and delivering a cohesive message to society about the seriousness of climate change and the imperative of taking action."

One could imagine an environmental group-only variant of such a Council focused on climate change, and indeed environmental NGOs have reportedly debated the potential value of such a coordinating body in recent years. Such a Council could usefully address some of the shortcomings discussed above by mitigating at least the most counter-productive forms of competition and forging a basis for coordinated action. Some, however, contend that this model of a loose Council would not be able to counteract the centrifugal forces diagnosed, and therefore that a new and more centralized organization is imperative. Making a Council successful will require a clear-eyed response to this concern. In the end, real tradeoffs will be required, including a major commitment from the organized environmental community to effect a large-scale shift of time, talent and money to the climate change issue and strong backing for this by foundations and other funders.

Many at our Conference, including major donors and foundation representatives, said that environmental organizations have simply not done a good enough job of working in partnership with each other on climate change – whether combining resources or crafting a common, mutually reinforcing, message on the issue.

Meanwhile, Conference Recommendation #36 seeks to correct for some of the limitations of the environmental groups we've discussed by ensuring that the new Council, if formed, would be cross-domain in composition right from the start – drawing in leaders from many segments of society beyond the environmental community.

DIFFUSION OF RESPONSIBILITY

After evaluating the incentives operating within each of the eight societal domains represented at the Conference, it is now worthwhile to reassemble the pieces and identify patterns cutting across them. Doing so yields the sobering insight that we are experiencing diffusion of responsibility on climate change. While no single individual or domain can plausibly be expected to take solitary charge on this encompassing problem, many who could assume leadership appears to think it is someone else's prerogative, or obligation, to do so. The result: a leadership vacuum.

Science and the Media

Evidence for the "diffusion of responsibility" thesis emerged most explicitly in the concurrent and then mixed discussions of scientists and news media professionals at the Conference. The scientists indicated that they and their peers are reticent at best about dancing with the media and, even when they are willing to try, often lack the media skills and training to do it effectively. Meanwhile, news media professionals said that they don't see it as an appropriate role for themselves to draw the scientists out or coach them on how to make their work on climate change more accessible or conventionally newsworthy. They express sympathy for the problem, but are deeply wary of being seen as conspiring with any subject, including scientists, to get their story in the media. Few, if any, see it as their job to do media training – that, they say, is what public relations firms are for.

Media and Politics

Furthermore, news media professionals admit that they are unlikely to move climate change out of the "ghetto" of their respective newspapers' science pages and put it on the political pages unless there are politicians championing the issue and generating a drumbeat of high-profile activity. Political leaders, for their part, are prone to follow the agenda-setting function of the news media: if a story is not already being covered with some volume and prominence, politicians are disinclined to respond to it and to instead favor topical issues that *are* being covered. Politicians see this as more than a matter of choice: their constituents expect them to comment and act on what they, in turn, are reading about in the media.

Business and Politics

Business leaders watch political leaders closely to anticipate and decode signals about their regulatory intentions on climate change and other issues. While the lack of national political leadership is frequently described as a key obstacle to meaningful action on climate change, some business leaders at the Conference noted that this predominant focus on the political vacuum may "let business off the hook" a bit too easily.

Meanwhile, political leaders are often unprepared to seize the initiative and move forward with a regulatory program if business leaders – particularly those in their district or on their donor rolls – have not indicated a comfort level with the affordability of that program. This dynamic may, for example, have prompted Massachusetts Governor Mitt Romney to back away from supporting the Regional Greenhouse Gas Initiative in late 2005 in the face of business concerns about its costs. (Note: the program moved forward without him as seven other Northeastern Governors signed a Memorandum of Understanding and launched the rule-making phase.) This political deference to business preferences has caused many to believe that until the business community signals a sufficiently broad readiness, the national government will not move forward on significant climate change policy action in the United States. So the path forward appears stymied by the "who goes first" problem.

Low-Carbon Products and the Chicken-or-Egg Problem

There is also a market-specific variant of the "diffusion of responsibility" phenomenon. This can be seen in the relationship between business and its customers with respect to low-carbon or carbon-neutral products, a consumer category that has not really taken off yet despite nascent efforts to sell "green energy" and "carbon offsets." The eight-principle framework discussed earlier (Recommendation #33) calls on business to educate its customers about climate change, specifically about "the carbon composition of products through websites, labels and bill stuffers, as it relates to the relevant business." This would require businesses to voluntarily disclose the climate change implications of their products and, in effect, create a market attribute by educating their customers. While businesses are attuned above all to their customers, participants at the Conference noted that, so far, few of them are hearing or experiencing demand from customers for low-carbon or no-carbon product offerings.

This presents an instance of the "chicken-or-egg" problem: Should businesses create a market or wait to respond to a market? Many Americans say on surveys that they are prepared to pay a little extra for environmental benefits (5-15 percent is one documented range for the "willingness-to-pay" premium, though a cautious distinction must be made between this stated willingness and actual behavior). Whether consumers will pay or not, a prior question is how often they even have the choice to buy a low-carbon or no-carbon product, reliably and clearly signified as such. If businesses wait for consumer demand to be expressed, they'll be waiting a long time because vehicles for expressing this demand are scarce.

This is not a unique case in the history of capitalism – businesses routinely need to decide how far to get out ahead of their customers. Occasionally, they take the risk of going beyond proven markets and launching a breakthrough product. The point, here, is that climate-neutral products are in this very chicken-or-egg zone right now. Will consumers become concerned enough about climate change to demand climate-friendly products and buy those few existing offerings that allow them to express this demand in sufficient volume to get the attention of businesses? Or will businesses decide to lead by launching climate-friendly products more broadly, labeled as such?

Businesses will be more inclined to lead and create the market once they're convinced their choice will be validated by consumer uptake and associated profits. This might even provide them with a differentiating advantage, which has long been a justification for eco-friendly branding.

But another approach is for an outside body to initiate a certification program and logo and then promote its adoption by businesses. This can become self-perpetuating once businesses realize they'll be at a competitive disadvantage if they do not sign on. Accordingly, Conference Recommendation #35 calls for the launch of a certification program and logo that would signify climate-friendly products. This has been undertaken on related issues, from EPA's Energy Star logo for energy-efficient appliances, which offers collateral benefits for climate change mitigation, to the Forest Stewardship Council, which certifies wood products that use sustainably harvested timber.

The recommendation recognizes, however, that there are also dozens of profit and not-for-profit entities already retailing "carbon offsets" or green energy produced from renewables. Some analysts have raised concerns about unevenness in the verification standards and quality of these offsets. For one thing, some of them are much stricter than others about administering "additionality" rules so that the offsets are genuinely incremental to what would occur on a business-as-usual basis — in other words, they really help address climate change. Relatedly, Renewable Energy Certificates (RECs) have often been incorrectly regarded as equivalent to carbon offsets, even though RECs are often issued to comply with state government mandates requiring a minimum of energy sourced from renewable sources – meaning that they may not be causing any additional reduction in greenhouse gas emissions beyond what would happen under business-as-usual regulatory compliance.

So while there is no shortage of emerging certification and logo efforts, there may be an opposite problem: too many of them, which diffuses resources across many initiatives rather than concentrating them on one or a few that could break through to attain consumer awareness. This proliferation of initiatives can simply be confusing to the consumer. Therefore, Recommendation #35 also calls for rationalizing these efforts and assessing their climate impacts. The result could be either launching a new and better one or spotlighting and combining the best of the existing ones.

Dialogue as an Antidote to Diffusion

One of the key benefits of our Conference format was that it permitted mutual and simultaneous recognition of inaction on a domain-by-domain basis. Put simply, it becomes harder to tell yourself that someone else will lead on climate change if you're in a room with them and they're looking back at you saying the same thing about you.

What this showed is that innovative dialogues can help counter the "diffusion of responsibility" phenomenon. Such dialogues will not always be enjoyable – to succeed, they probably need to contain explicit and uncomfortable discussions about past buck-passing as well as a readiness by all participants to consider expanding the boundary of their responsibilities at a time when Americans are already famously time-starved. Unlike many of the Conference recommendations calling for the launching of campaigns or new entities, the diffusion of responsibility problem requires a more open-ended type of activity in the form of organic, unscripted, and authentic dialogues *between people who don't normally connect*. The organizers of these dialogues must be prepared to let unpredictable dynamics unfold. Some of the proposed dialogues should be public, others private.

Along the way toward new assumptions of responsibility, such dialogues could help break down the long-standing stereotypes so prevalent in debates about environmental issues today. E.O. Wilson, in writing about the lack of public will to tackle the biodiversity problem, has lamented "the total-war portraits crafted for public consumption by extremists on both sides" (Edward O. Wilson, *The Future of Life*: 152). Yet he suggests that they are not an insuperable barrier to success: "The stereotypes cannot be simply dismissed, since they are so often voiced and contain elements of real substance . . . But they can be understood clearly and sidestepped in the search for common ground" (ibid).

The Conference recommended a number of dialogues and interfaces (religion-business; religion-science; science-news media through the bridging institution, etc.) that could help counter the diffusion of responsibility and create new kinds of connective tissue in our society in relation to climate change. Moreover, there is no reason to limit future such meetings to the permutations recommended by the Conference. Nearly every one of the domains represented at our Conference could usefully meet bilaterally or in multi-domain groups, as well as with other domains that were not represented – all with a focus on finding new forms of collaboration on climate change, and clarifying who will lead.

Put simply, it becomes harder to tell yourself that someone else will lead on climate change if you're in a room with them and they're looking back at you saying the same thing about you.

One of the participants who joined us in Aspen looked back on the Conference with a couple months hindsight and said, echoing Marshall McLuhan, that the "meeting was the message" – meaning that the diverse assemblage of representatives from different segments of our society working together to candidly diagnose their own accountabilities for a major problem, and to propose remedies, was unusual and inspirational. Indeed, the Conference modeled a kind of integrative behavior that often seems scarce in an era of heightened partisanship and specialization. This participant suggested that "mini-Aspens" could usefully be convened around the country, modeled loosely on our Conference and drawing in a diverse group of predominantly local representatives to address climate change.

New Coordinating Mechanisms to Counter Diffusion

Dialogue can serve as an important catalyst to joint understandings and action – while no panacea, its status in our solution set should be regarded as secure. Dialogues that recur over time may, as well, become candidates for at least loose institutionalization, as in the multi-domain Leadership Council discussed earlier (Recommendation #36).

The enormity of the climate change issue and the need for action on all levels precludes a single, umbrella-style approach to coordinating all concerned individuals and entities in America. It would simply be too unwieldy. But in a tacit admission that the different elements of American society have not played "team ball" in addressing climate change to date, the Conference recommended that new kinds of coordination be tried. These range from the bridging institution that would coordinate and translate scientists' voices on climate change science (Recommendation #1) to the proposal for a new overarching communications entity that would help overcome the fragmented communications efforts on the issue to date (Recommendation #25).

In each case, the Conference participants debated whether a new entity is required or whether existing ones should be augmented. Building a new entity can be a resource sink and a way to defer real action. And, of course, any development plan for a new entity must begin with a thorough evaluation of the capabilities of existing entities that currently perform some part of the newly proposed mandate. For example, how distinct is the proposed Leadership Council from the existing Apollo Alliance, a broad coalition that has formed a 10-point plan to produce 3 million new jobs while promoting adoption of clean energy that reduces greenhouse gas emissions? The American Association for the Advancement of Science and other organizations, including advocacy-oriented NGOs with a scientific focus, already perform some of the key functions of the proposed bridging institution, though rarely with a singular climate change focus.

Duplication must be minimized. At the same time, the very real bureaucratic obstacles and other challenges of kick-starting new initiatives within existing institutions must also be acknowledged.

Along the spectrum from the loose coordination of a council to a centralized institution exist many intermediate formats capable of enhancing the level of societal coordination on the climate change issue. Recommendation #29, for example, calls for a mechanism that could allow strategic diversity to flourish while also providing the minimum required level of coordination so that the various strategies being pursued might cumulate to a larger total impact. It urges the organization of a mass grassroots educational campaign to create specifically local narratives around climate change impacts and solutions. An important strategic innovation embedded in this recommendation would be to initiate the campaign with a National Climate Week that would recur on an annual basis, possibly in September during the hurricane season. This week would then serve as a focal period of activity, which would reduce the burden of top-down orchestration of the grassroots campaign since all organizations could be urged to independently plan events during this week but otherwise be left largely to their own devices.

THE AFFLICTION OF PARTISANSHIP

Climate change is a partisan issue in today's America. The policy stalemate in Washington, D.C. has left those committed to action uncertain about whether a partisan or bipartisan strategy is more likely to succeed going forward. For all its direct costs, partisanship has also had profound spillover effects, chilling public engagement on climate change throughout our society and compelling many people to take sides instead of collaborating to craft policies and actions as warranted by the science.

This report has already touched on the issue of partisanship, but it is so critical to explaining the science action gap that it deserves its own thematic category. It has also discussed other important societal divisions that could usefully be bridged, such as that between the religious community and scientists. But the division between our political parties, at both the leadership and rank-and-file levels, is clearly one of the deepest fault lines in today's America. It is impeding societal action on climate change and many other issues on which we can ill afford delay.

Despite glimmers of bipartisanship in the U.S. Senate and in some Statehouses, climate change today remains the subject of a long-running stalemate. The direct costs of partisanship are displayed most flamboyantly in the theater of Washington, D.C., where even tentative forward steps, such as the McCain-Lieberman Climate Stewardship Act, have been held up for years. Partisanship has, by most accounts, grown more intense and uncivil in recent years. If this can be reduced, whether by a natural down-cycle or some intentional campaign to boost civic responsibility among elected officials – at least on the issues where we can least afford it – it could go a long way toward advancing progress on climate change.

When Did Climate Change Become a Partisan Issue?

The story of partisanship and climate change is a topic that deserves more analysis and probably book-length treatment to answer fully. But it is worth exploring a key inflection point from our recent past. Partisanship on the issue intensified during the 1997 debate over the Kyoto Protocol, according to an important study conducted by political scientist Jon Krosnick, a participant at our Conference (see Krosnick et al., "The Impact of the Fall 1997 Debate About Global Warming on American Public Opinion," *Public Understanding of Science*, Vol. 9, No. 3, 2000: 239-260).

The Clinton Administration initiated a concentrated campaign to build support for the Kyoto Protocol on October 6, 1997, at the White House Conference on Global Climate Change. Krosnick's content analysis documents how the volume of media coverage intensified during the October-December period of that year, in tandem with the Administration push. Interestingly, polling of Americans before and after this period shows that the percentages of Americans who believed global warming was occurring (77 percent), would continue to occur (74 percent), was a bad thing (61 percent) and constituted a serious or very serious problem (32 percent) stayed roughly the same.

Underneath this aggregate stability, however, Krosnick found that the debate had dramatically polarized the population by party, not just in terms of preferred policies but also perceptions of the problem's scientific validity.

Before the Clinton Administration push and associated media coverage, for example, the percentage of strong Democrats who thought global warming was happening (73 percent) was only slightly higher than the number of strong Republicans who thought so (68 percent) – a 5 percent gap. Afterward, this 5 percent gap surged to 18 percent. This pattern was replicated on other questions.

Other more recent data shows that the partisan gap has persisted on the issue of climate change. Steven Kull's 2005 PIPA survey found that 62 percent of Democrats perceived a scientific consensus on climate change, as compared to just 41 percent of Republicans.

Before the Clinton Administration push and associated media coverage, for example, the percentage of strong Democrats who thought global warming was happening (73 percent) was only slightly higher than the number of strong Republicans who thought so (68 percent) – a 5 percent gap. Afterward, this 5 percent gap surged to 18 percent. This pattern was replicated on other questions.

An important question here is whether attitude change is stickier in the opposite direction: once an issue has become polarized, can that polarization be reduced on roughly the same timeline, or a faster one? How would one accomplish this? By varying the partisan identification of the key messengers, for example? This and other mechanisms can and should be tested through research in political science, psychology and other social sciences.

Strategic Uncertainty: Pursue a Partisan or Bipartisan Approach?

Concerted efforts to reduce the polarization, however, will likely only proceed if there is sufficient agreement among party leaders that doing so is worthwhile. Interestingly, it appears that such agreement may not exist.

A key strategic problem on climate change, then, is not only the partisanship itself, but disagreement about how best to respond to it. At the Conference, we witnessed forceful disagreement between those who prefer to treat climate change as a partisan issue and others who see the path forward as one of bipartisan compromise. Each approach suggests distinct strategies.

The partisan strategy calls for articulating and perhaps expanding the distinction between the parties on climate change, and then harnessing the issue to draw votes, achieve victory, and eventually establish a mandate to assert one's preferred policy over the objections of the other party.

A bipartisan strategy, on the other hand, would suggest formulating a middle-ground policy approach that compromises enough on both sides to establish a basis for near-term legislative advancements on climate change.

A key strategic problem on climate change, then, is not only the partisanship itself, but disagreement about how best to respond to it. At the Conference, we witnessed forceful disagreement between those who prefer to treat climate change as a partisan issue and others who see the path forward as one of bipartisan compromise. Each approach suggests distinct strategies.

Which is more feasible? Which is more likely to attain meaningful outcomes in terms of actually mitigating climate change? (Unfortunately the answers to these two questions often diverge.)

The proponents of the partisan approach note that this issue has become so intractably aligned with the partisan divide that any concessions are unlikely to be reciprocated, resulting in further marginalization of the climate change issue. Instead, they say the only way to proceed is to exercise raw political power, wake up the public about the urgent nature of the issue, create a major public demand for action comparable to that which stimulated major environmental legislation in the 1970s, pursue outright victory at the polls, and prompt a general realignment in Washington, D.C.

Those favoring a bipartisan approach, on the other hand, prefer to separate the climate change issue from any partisan agenda so that the first and most feasible steps toward meaningful action can be passed into law at the earliest possible date – some call this a "purple" strategy (i.e., blending blue states and red states). The bipartisan roots of environmental progress are seen as favoring this model, and spotlighting that history to the rank-and-file is seen as one way to mobilize bipartisan support today.

While the Conference participants were not asked to reach consensus, the prevailing sentiment seemed to favor the bipartisan model. This became explicit in the case of the "New Vision for Energy" Recommendation (#20), which many thought would attain its goals more readily if bipartisan support for it were cultivated.

But the preference for bipartisanship at the Conference was not unconditional. Pursuit of bipartisan legislation on climate change that is capable of passage in both chambers of the U.S. Congress, perhaps an elusive goal in today's power configuration, should not be permitted to devolve into a recipe for minimalist or token goals. Rather, any such legislation should be calibrated according to scientific evidence of what emissions reductions are needed, and over what time frame. Ultimately, testing the "bipartisan possible" against the science is the most intellectually honest way to choose between a bipartisan and partisan strategy. If the bipartisan bill that proves feasible is patently inadequate, it might still be pursued as a transient tactical maneuver, but this should not thereby rule out pursuit of a sharper partisan strategy and a robust civic engagement strategy if that is what is ultimately required to generate action that is commensurate with the science.

Spillover Effects Chill the Societal Dialogue

Perhaps the most underrated consequence of partisanship is that the aura of controversy it creates has seeped far beyond Washington D.C. and chilled our society's overall engagement with the climate change issue, in ways large and small.

This starts at the cocktail-party level. Many people are conflict-averse, and in polite company, they instinctively avoid raising issues that have partisan content because of the risk of damaging relationships between family members or friends. Climate change appears to have fallen into this category of risky issues, which impedes the flow of information and the values-based dialogues that might otherwise occur. A lack of cocktail chatter may seem like a trivial matter, but if one substitutes enough dysfunctional silences where conversation might otherwise have occurred, the vibrancy of our democracy is undermined and our ability to contend with issues like climate change is compromised.

Moving to the workplace, many Americans are prohibited by the tax-exempt status of their organizations (or other dictates of protocol or decorum), from lobbying and, more importantly, are discouraged from saying anything that might even be perceived as such. In this way, also, partisanship and controversy cast a long shadow. School teachers reportedly exhibit reluctance to teach the issue for fear it will provoke the ire of parents. Climate scientists risk character assassination – and possibly their funding – if they enter the public domain and speak out on the public policy implications of their findings.

The politicization of the climate change issue has also reverberated through the business community. We heard at the Conference that some business leaders have been privately told not to take a forthcoming stance on the issue by elected officials who are important to their ability to get things done, such as the issuance of permits for new facilities. Some noted that this begins to sound like a sort of "upside down" democracy, where politicians are lobbying their constituents rather than the other way around.

Defusing Partisanship – At Least on Climate Change

The Conference did not presume to solve the issue of partisanship in America, but did pose several ways to potentially detach the issue of climate change from the larger stalemate.

➢ First, it recommended a purple strategy to promote transformation of our nation's energy system (Recommendation #20). This report has discussed the compelling argument that the ongoing reevaluation of U.S. energy strategy may be the best wagon to which the climate change issue could be hitched, provided the cautions mentioned earlier are heeded.

➢ Second, given the problems of taking partisanship head-on, Recommendation #23 calls for a work-around whereby party elders no longer in office would convene to explore and develop areas of common ground on the climate change issue. Then, and only then, they would privately caucus with incumbents in their respective parties to seek to ameliorate the partisan dynamic at play on the climate change issue.

➢ Third, two other recommendations viewed religion and morality as pivotal to shaking up the partisan entrenchment on climate change. Recommendation #14 urges that the religious community communicate the urgency of addressing climate change to the nation's political leadership and Recommendation #21 advises that climate change be "recast" as a "moral and faith issue, not a scientific or environmental one," and that a broader coalition of allies be catalyzed "around this moral common ground."

SETTING GOALS

> *Those working to promote societal action on climate change need to do a better job of formulating goals that are capable of promoting convergent strategies by dispersed and often uncoordinated actors, and commensurate with a real solution to the problem. In order to guide and motivate needed actions, these goals should be generated collaboratively, scientifically calibrated, quantifiable, trackable and easily expressible. They should include not only emissions targets but also, given the crucial importance of "public will," attitudinal targets.*

We found among the Conference participants a widespread view that those working to promote action on climate change can and must do better in coordinating their efforts around common goals. There are acknowledged exceptions that are handling the goal-setting task with admirable skill. For example, the 25 x 25 initiative discussed earlier has coordinated a coalition of interests around the quantified and easily expressible goal of having U.S. agriculture provide 25 percent of the total energy consumed in the United States by 2025. Meanwhile, 219 American cities (and counting) have pledged to fulfill the Kyoto Protocol's emissions reductions target, in recognition of the value of a salient and widely referenced policy goal over a customized one. Policy advocates have, for years now, coordinated around the policy goal of passing the McCain–Lieberman Climate Stewardship Act in the Senate to institute a cap-and-trade program to limit greenhouse gas emissions to 2000 levels by 2010. Others have worked for decades to raise CAFE standards for automotive fuel efficiency.

These continuing efforts deserve support from those concerned about climate change. But they arguably have limitations as the basis for a sufficiently broad and long-term strategy for the nation, either because they are sector-specific (agriculture or automotive), too short-term (Kyoto expires in 2012 unless extended), too incremental to be scientifically defensible, etc.

An integrated national goal could indeed package and build on the best of these ongoing efforts. But to get to a robust national goal that has the features described above will require more by way of cross-domain dialogue that reflects and reconciles science, values, economics, communications and all the other considerations covered above.

The fact is that meaningful differences remain in the nature and stringency of goals advocated by those concerned about climate change.

In some cases, this appears to be a function of key stakeholders not having enough information – scientific, economic and otherwise – to judge what an appropriate goal should be, or an ability to integrate these types of information.

One reason that goal-setting among those working on climate change is often untethered from science is that most scientists have been reluctant to speak out or to impose what they see as value judgments by declaring certain levels of emissions as "dangerous." Exceptions include prominent NASA scientist James Hansen who has recently said that if we do not keep additional warming under 1° Centigrade (1.8° Fahrenheit), we may cross dangerous tipping points. His estimate is that this implies a window of 10 years to begin significant emissions reductions. The White House has allegedly sought to restrict Hansen's outspokenness, a controversy that has drawn much media coverage including a March 2006 story on *60 Minutes*.

A second key challenge impeding the application of science to goal-setting is that data on the impacts of climate change are still incomplete, often unquantifiable and difficult to link to specific greenhouse gas stabilization targets. The IPCC's report in 2001 conceded that ". . . comprehensive, quantitative estimates of the benefits of stabilization at various levels of atmospheric greenhouse gases do not yet exist." Moreover, the impacts data that *do* exist are rarely organized around time frames that map to the needs of policy-makers aiming to specify a path of emissions targets.

Without such "bright lines" supplied by the scientists, other factors – especially economic or political feasibility – tend to drive goal-setting.

The Four Paradoxes of Urgency

A recurring theme among those seeking to create "public will" and action on climate change is that of "urgency."

Urgency is an inherently subjective concept and yet a pivotal one given that it often mediates the connection between intention and behavior. What is it? It is a condition or sensation associated with a "pressing necessity" (American Heritage Dictionary). It is one of those "know it when you see it (or feel it)" concepts. Those who sense the urgency of climate change are impatient for action. Those who don't sense the urgency don't get what all the fuss is about. So how "urgent" is the public about climate change?

Steven Kull's 2005 PIPA poll found that a full 76 percent of Americans believe that global warming is a problem that requires action, with only 21 percent opposing any steps with economic costs. But he also found a significant split on the matter of perceived urgency: 42 percent of the total said the effect of global warming "will be gradual, so we can deal with the problem gradually by taking steps that are low in cost," and 34 percent said the problem is "pressing" and "we should begin taking steps now even if this involves significant costs."

A June 2005, ABC-Washington Post poll revealed substantially the same findings: "Nearly six in 10 Americans think global warming likely is underway and as many accept that human activities play a significant role. But – like the Bush Administration – most part company with scientists' calls for prompt action. That lack of urgency stems from perceptions of the hazards: While a vast majority, nearly eight in 10 believe global warming will pose a serious threat to future generations, far fewer – just one-third – think it'll affect their own lives. The majority who see the risk as a distant one overwhelmingly prefer more study to immediate action." The poll also noted that only 38 percent of Americans view global warming as an "urgent problem that required immediate government action." At least four paradoxes associated with urgency are worth considering.

Paradox #1: How to Be Urgent About the Unknown

A major wild card in society's calculations on climate change is the potential for non-linear climatic surprises ahead. Scientists broadly agree that the climate system is unpredictable and rife with unknown thresholds, that it can flip like a switch from one state to another in abbreviated periods and that we do not – and probably *cannot* – develop precise estimates of the likelihood and timing of such events.

One of the most prominent such scenarios is a potential weakening or collapse of the thermohaline circulation that brings warm Gulf water to the North Atlantic and keeps especially Western Europe habitable. But there are many others. Scientists have increasingly expressed surprise about the acceleration of certain events, from the collapse of the massive Larsen B ice shelf on the Antarctic Peninsula over a 35-day period starting in January 2002 to more recent NASA satellite observations indicating the quickening of the melting of the Greenland ice sheet. In 2005, scientists returning from a massive Siberian peat bog indicated that its permafrost layer was melting rapidly and could release enormous quantities of trapped methane, a potent greenhouse gas (the west Siberian bog alone is estimated to contain approximately 70 billion tons of methane, a quarter of all the methane stored on the land surface worldwide). Other scientists are now assessing how acidification of the oceans from absorption of carbon dioxide may imperil the viability of ocean life.

Some economists argue that we need only take gradual action to reduce emissions since, by their calculations, the marginal costs of investing in near-term emissions mitigation outweigh the present value of net future benefits and costs delivered for that investment. Putting aside intractable debates about the right discount rate, this line of argument typically moves too quickly past the issue of non-linear surprises. Some simply dismiss such scenarios as "not probable." This omits that many of these scenarios are not improbable either. Scientists often refrain from assigning probabilities to non-linear scenarios because probabilistic methods are not appropriate for some of them and the models are not equipped to predict them.

So given all this, we have something of a paradox. It is difficult to create urgency about avoiding something unknown and unknowable – and to craft communications that motivate action on this diffuse basis. And yet, as far as we know, we may be currently and inadvertently crossing thresholds we do not recognize – entraining irreversible consequences.

The "precautionary principle" asserts that we should err on the side of caution in the face of this uncertainty, but this principle has not shown a capacity to galvanize public will to date.

It is difficult to create urgency about avoiding something unknown and unknowable – and to craft communications that motivate action on this diffuse basis. And yet, as far as we know, we may be currently and inadvertently crossing thresholds we do not recognize – entraining irreversible consequences.

Urgency is difficult enough to generate on any problem characterized by cause-effect time lags, but this challenge is compounded with climate change because the lags are themselves of uncertain duration and the severity of the consequences at intervals along the way still poorly understood.

Conference Recommendation #2 seeks to address the impact of this information limitation, to the extent possible, by urging that research priorities on climate change be reoriented to "be more responsive to society's information and decision-making needs" including greater emphasis on non-linear consequences and feedbacks that could inform society's level of urgency on climate change.

Paradox #2: Urgency Is a Relational Function Between Science and Power Plants

Even if potential non-linear impacts could be quantified and projected, this would not complete our equation. That is because urgency, when translated from a sensation to action, is not only about the science but about the timing of investment decisions and the inertia of our capital infrastructure.

The lock-in of investments in long-lived centralized energy infrastructure assets will commit us to decades of rising emissions from those sources, putting aside the unpalatable option of premature retirement of capital down the line. This is obvious to many who work on the climate change issue or in the energy industry. Yet it has been the source of epiphanies for powerful leaders seeking to calculate the relative urgency of action on climate change.

A quick anecdote illuminates the point. One leader in the "carbon finance" arena described a private meeting with an elected official who is active in the legislative maneuvering on climate change. In the course of that conversation, the official had an epiphany that intensified his sense of urgency.

The turning point was the financier's mention of ongoing plans to construct nearly 120 traditional pulverized coal-fired power plants in the U.S. alone over the coming years (sending U.S. coal use up at least 40 percent over the next twenty-plus years). China reportedly has plans to construct four to five times that number. These plans create a surprisingly narrow window of opportunity to act if one wants to reduce emissions.

Note that this urgency-inducing information is about investment cycles. As such, it is distinct from scientific information about what greenhouse gas concentrations and near-term pathways may be "dangerous." In other words, the urgency equation requires inputs of both kinds to produce an appropriate answer. It is about matches and mismatches between the dictates of science and the dynamics of capital formation and deployment over time.

Some at the Conference reported having heard others in the business community say they're "deeply concerned" about the climate change issue and "when it starts happening, we'll address it." This sentiment misses on two scores: it fails to grasp the time-lagged nature of climate change and, just as problematically, the tight relationship of the science to the lock-in problem associated with infrastructure and other inertial drivers of our society's greenhouse gas emissions.

Paradox #3: Communicating Urgency Explicitly May Diminish Urgency

As discussed earlier, social psychologists have documented how people filter and discount messages they receive based on various attributes of the messenger, such as perceived trustworthiness and knowledgeability, not to mention cultural, gender, attractiveness and other traits. In separate strands of inquiry, scholars study the persuasiveness of the messages themselves, independent of the messenger. Then they explore how the interactive effects between the messenger and the message influence the listener.

At the Conference, we heard anecdotal evidence, pending more rigorous verification, that messages of *urgent* concern may be even more heavily filtered and discounted than messages lacking that feature, particularly if delivered by distrusted messengers. One religious leader indicated that messages of "urgency" on climate change often provoke a backlash among his constituents. Urgency is especially prone to being discounted as unreasoned alarmism or even passion.

Climate change is an issue that is so grand in its scope and consequences that it can become identity-defining for those most involved in advocating on it. In the aftermath of a 20th century defined by ideological extremism and movements, many Americans today have an understandable suspicion of any and all claims of urgent needs for societal transformations (including to rapidly reduce greenhouse gas emissions), as well as to those who advocate most passionately for them.

What this suggests, paradoxically then, is that the best way to generate urgency may not always be to explicitly or overtly communicate urgency. Urgency may instead be a condition or sensation that people must internally generate. Trying to impose it on them may, at least in some cases, be counterproductive.

This likely varies based on the trustworthiness of the messenger, but at this point we are speculating – further social science research is needed.

Paradox #4: Which Comes First: The Urgency or the Goal?

Should "urgency" drive goal-setting or be derived from the goal once its attendant demands are clear? Urgency is an imprecise and elastic guide to action, one that is difficult to operationalize:

> ➤ urgency can mean that we must get started now on emissions reductions, at whatever stringency level is feasible to negotiate and implement – the key is just to get going.

> ➤ urgency can mean that we must put a binding long-term plan in place now, even if the early-year targets are lenient and the stringent targets do not hit until many years out.

> ➤ urgency can mean that we must, now at last, grasp the true dimension of the climate change challenge and undertake a bold rethinking that will disdain incremental steps and be steadfastly unsatisfied with anything less than substantial emissions reductions commensurate with the science, including a safe margin for error.

The common denominator across these meanings is that something is expected to happen now, but this says little about exactly what that is. Urgency does influence the strategic instruments one will be inclined to favor. For example, those with a sense of urgency will, even if they have not formulated specific goals, tend to favor the Conference recommendations calling for advertising campaigns over slower-burning education initiatives.

Recognizing the catalytic power of a sense of urgency, Conference Recommendation #6 calls for the convening of "one or more dialogues free of economic and political compromises to undertake a fundamental redefinition of the climate change challenge in light of its urgency."

This recommendation implicitly says that we are now boxed into an overly narrow set of concepts, assumptions, and feasibility calculations. By assembling those who have different perspectives on the urgency of climate change and different views about the right next step, new frames of reference could be developed and convergent actions identified.

Such dialogues could be highly useful, as long as they conclude by circling back to the core organizing need of specifying an actionable goal. While our Conference did not seek to attain consensus on appropriate national goals, its recommendations call for fostering a number of venues where disciplined goal-setting could usefully be undertaken with the right stakeholders and processes.

Given its importance, some general points and context on goal-setting will now be provided, distinguishing between emissions-reduction targets and attitudinal targets.

Emissions Reduction Targets

In formulating climate change goals, we are naturally inclined to start with "targets and timetables" for emissions reductions (and allow for market-based trading to reduce overall compliance costs) since this has become the dominant strategy in the global response to climate change to date.

This "cap-and-trade" model is embodied in the Kyoto Protocol, which imposes an aggregate reduction target of 5.2 percent below 1990 levels averaged over the 5-year period 2008-2012, with each country's target varying based on case-by-case negotiations.

Within this basic framework, there are many other design options and variations to consider (for example, sector-by-sector targets or emissions-intensity reductions indexed on a per unit of GDP or per capita basis, rather than caps on absolute emissions), but these are beyond the purview of this report.

Given our focus in this Conference on the U.S., it is also worth noting that the U.S. government has continued to refrain from ratifying the Kyoto Protocol and instead announced on July 28, 2005, an alternative technology development and diffusion strategy that forgoes any overarching cap on emissions. Known as the Asia Pacific Partnership on Clean Development and Climate, it includes Australia, India, Japan, the People's Republic of China, South Korea, and the United States.

Against that background, our Conference did not spend a great deal of time debating different emissions target levels as a whole. But the Business & Finance group's eight-principle framework included a goal that we will unpack here to illuminate the context and issues associated with goal-setting on climate change (Recommendation #33). The group's goal reads: "Support a long-term goal for global greenhouse gas emissions from all segments of the U.S. economy at or below today's levels by 2050." This goal is:

➤ pegged to 2005 emissions as a baseline, which is somewhat less stringent than the Kyoto Protocol's 1990 baseline, when emissions were lower.

➤ a longer-term target than Kyoto, thereby following most leading policy-designers working on climate change in recognizing that a vital attribute of an effective goal on this issue is that it be long-term. As S. Pacala and R. Socolow put it, in favoring a mid-century target: "The next 50 years is a sensible horizon from several perspectives. It is the length of a career, the life-time of a power plant, and an interval for which the technology is close enough to envision" (*Science* Vol. 305, No. 5686: 968).

➤ a point-year emissions target that leaves open what the emissions path and interim targets between now and 2050 should be, though the implication is that one would want to avoid significant increases in the meantime since that would force deeper reductions later, as 2050 approaches.

> ➤ ambiguous, and therefore open to a crucial negotiation, on whether 2050 emissions should be held to today's levels or reduced, potentially by the 60 percent or greater amount that many experts now believe will be needed by that time (see more on this below).

> ➤ silent on what should happen after 2050, whereas many experts contend that the second half of the century will need to be a period of significantly reduced emissions, converging on net zero emissions, if we are to stabilize concentrations in the atmosphere, rather than simply add to them at a level rate.

While our entire Conference, and this goal, intentionally focused on the U.S., we should note that a major challenge ahead is how to ensure inclusion of all major emitting countries – including developing countries – in a climate change goal, since failure to do so will not solve the problem. That, of course, is the most famous oversight in the Kyoto Protocol, which served as a fatal Achilles heel for its opponents to exploit in domestic advertisements that said, to great apparent effect: "It's not global and it won't work."

Various ingenious models for bridging developing countries into a post-Kyoto compliance regime have been advanced by experts in market-based mechanisms such as Robert Stavins of Harvard University and others. They include, for example, proposals through which developing countries would incur increasingly stringent emissions reductions targets at trigger points along the trajectory of their increases in average per capita income. This would allow them an allocation of atmospheric capacity sufficient to advance their developmental needs over time, while eventually bringing them into line with the global imperative to stabilize concentrations.

The present U.S. Administration has objected to the Kyoto Protocols as draconian. Indeed, given the emissions growth since 1990 (2004 emissions in the U.S. were 15.8 percent above 1990 levels), achieving the Kyoto targets in the short time remaining would be difficult, if not as economically damaging as the Administration has contended. As a reference point, Canada, which has ratified the Kyoto Protocol has also experienced rapid economic growth since 1990 and seen its emissions rise 24 percent. It is now struggling with how to comply with its Kyoto obligation, and some say that its failure is all but inevitable.

What is striking, then, is that the Kyoto targets are both challenging and, in scientific terms, inadequate. Those who have advocated for Kyoto ratification and compliance have therefore been in the uncomfortable position of calling for a costly solution that won't solve the problem. Robert Stavins' verdict on Kyoto: "Too little, too fast."

On the other hand, the proverbial journey of a thousand miles begins with the first step and the Kyoto Protocol is directionally correct, unlike our current business-as-usual trajectory toward ever-growing emissions. Had U.S. ratification occurred soon after its 1997 completion, Kyoto would have entered into force much sooner than February 2005. U.S. ratification, moreover, would have sent a signal to its domestic market, the most entrepreneurial in the world, and we would have been on a lower emissions path. Furthermore, earlier ratification of the Kyoto Protocol would have meaningfully underscored the seriousness of the industrialized world about addressing climate change, potentially drawing developing country participation into the next phase. Kyoto was not designed to "work" in terms of solving the problem by itself – its very timetable makes clear that it was but a first step.

As it is, the post-Kyoto regime is now a matter of great suspense, and the latest round of negotiations – at the Montreal "Conference of the Parties" in December 2005 – was ambiguous in terms of building confidence that the world is on track for an effective goal-setting effort on climate change.

What is striking, then, is that the Kyoto targets are both challenging and, in scientific terms, inadequate. Those who have advocated for Kyoto ratification and compliance have therefore been in the uncomfortable position of calling for a costly solution that won't solve the problem. Robert Stavins' verdict on Kyoto: "Too little, too fast."

What should the goal be? Experts usually start from a maximum acceptable temperature increase consistent with minimizing the risks of a wide range of damages, and work back from that to atmospheric concentration levels for greenhouse gases that would, based on current modeling, be likely to keep temperatures under that targeted ceiling.

If we stay on a business-as-usual trajectory, the scenarios from the Intergovernmental Panel on Climate Change show atmospheric concentrations rising anywhere from 90 percent to 250 percent (i.e., 530 to 970 parts per million) over the benchmark pre-industrial level of 280 parts per million by the year 2100. (The current concentration is approximately 381 parts per million.)

In 2005, the European Union formally reaffirmed its view that the global mean temperature increase should not exceed 2° Centigrade (3.6° Fahrenheit). Models indicate that preventing this level of temperature increases will require stabilization of carbon dioxide levels at somewhere between 450 and 550 parts per million by 2100, or less than a "doubling" of the pre-industrial level. But this remains a probabilistic game complete with bands of uncertainty and unknown triggers that could cause abrupt climate changes along the way.

So given this stabilization goal and its associated uncertainties, then the issue turns to what the pathway to that goal should be (i.e., how stringent should the near term targets be, and what is the extended time-path of targets thereafter?).

One of the most thoughtful discussions of the need to begin greenhouse gas emissions reductions without further delay (and by how much to reduce them) can be found in Malte Meinshausen et al., "Multi-Gas Emission Pathways to Meet Climate Targets" (*Climatic Change*, Vol. 5, No. 1-2, March 2006). Consistent with our earlier discussion about the limited dissemination of scientific findings, it is probably safe to assume that most readers of the present report do not have this issue of *Climatic Change* on their bedside table, so we reprint the conclusion of this important article here, with emphases added:

> "Achieving climate targets that account for, say, the risk of disintegrating ice sheets (Oppenheimer, 1998; Hansen, 2003; Oppenheimer and Alley, 2004) or for large scale extinction risks (Thomas et al., 2004) *almost certainly requires substantial and near term emission reductions. For example, to constrain global-mean temperatures to peaking at 2° C above the pre-industrial level with reasonable certainty (say > 75%) would require emission reductions of the order of 60% below 1990 levels by 2050* for the GWP-weighted sum of all greenhouse gases . . . If the start of significant emission reductions were further delayed, the necessary rates of emissions reduction rates were even higher, if the risk of overshooting certain temperature levels shouldn't be increased (den Elzen and Meinshausen, 2005; Meinshausen, 2005).

> Thus, since more rapid reductions may require the premature retirement of existing capital stocks, the cost of any further delay would be increased, probably non-linearly. There are a number of other reasons why one might want to avoid further

delay. Firstly, future generations face more stringent emission reductions while already facing increased costs of climate impacts. Secondly, the potential benefits of 'learning by doing' (Arrow, 1962; Gritsevskyi and Nakicenovi, 2000; Grubb and Ulph, 2002) were limited due to the more sudden deployment of new technology and infrastructure. Thirdly, *a further delay of mitigation efforts risks the potential foreclosure of reaching certain climate targets.* Thus, a delay might be particularly costly if, for example, the climate sensitivity turns out to be towards the higher end of the currently assumed ranges (cf. Andronova and Schlesinger, 2001: Forest et al., 2002: Knutti et al., 2003)."

Let us first acknowledge that this excerpt, while authoritative, is not emblematic of the accessible language we must increasingly see in communications to the general public about climate change goals. This is a journal article intended primarily for scientists and other inside specialists. Someone needs to translate and carry this kind of work to key constituencies and the general public – see Conference Recommendation #1 calling for a bridging institution capable of fulfilling this need.

Meanwhile, in interpreting the authors' bracing conclusion, it is worth noting that even the +2° C global average warming (+3.6° F) ceiling cited here may prove too lenient to prevent ice sheet melting, widespread coral bleaching, ecosystem disruption, agricultural losses and other adverse consequences. That +2° C rise would be over three times the warming experienced in the 20th century.

Moreover, the 60 percent reduction by 2050 called for here is a globally averaged reduction target. The industrial countries, and especially the United States, would, in all likelihood, have to make deeper cuts to allow for inevitable acceleration of developing country emissions. Thus, the long-term target announced by California Governor Arnold Schwarzenegger in June 2005 to reduce emissions of greenhouse gases to 80 percent below 1990 levels by 2050 is close to what could be expected for the United States as a whole under the prescriptions advanced in the article.

As noted earlier, the February 2006 U.S. EPA draft of the National Emissions Inventory estimates that U.S. emissions grew 15.8 percent from 1990-2004, so any targeted cuts *below 1990 levels*, as called for above, would need to account for the fact that we are already well above 1990 levels today – further compounding the reductions that would be needed.

Of course, the relative urgency of undertaking near-term emissions reductions in line with this article's conclusion is not without controversy. For example, some economists have argued that the optimal emissions reductions plan is to start modestly. Then, if damages rise more quickly in the future than expected, stringency can be tightened. In this view, short-term targets are often favored over long-term ones since it is posited that humanity can learn in the interim and shouldn't foreclose future options. One might counter that this does not account adequately for the path-dependence of our emissions trajectory and the likelihood that future reduction costs will be higher once high-emitting infrastructure is locked in. Moreover, in the absence of long-term targets, and the price signal they send, businesses may lack the regulatory predictability needed to guide long-term capital budgeting, including investments in low-carbon infrastructure.

Meanwhile, in interpreting the authors' bracing conclusion, it is worth noting that even the +2° C global average warming (+3.6° F) ceiling cited here may prove too lenient to prevent ice sheet melting, widespread coral bleaching, ecosystem disruption, agricultural losses and other adverse consequences. That +2° C rise, incidentally, would be over three times the warming experienced in the 20th century.

Another line of argument from those advocating modest rather than urgent action is based on studies showing potential benefits of climate change at certain latitudes, usually in polar and mid-latitude regions, at least up to 2.5° C (4.5° F) of warming in the latter case, with damages expected to set in if temperatures go higher than that. These methodologies frequently sum up these potential benefits with warming-induced damages in other regions, such as the sub-tropics. One might counter that it is simplistic to sum positives and negatives across geographies like this. Won't sub-tropical damages cause global ramifications, environmentally and socially, including for those living at latitudes supposedly benefitting from the changes (mass immigration pressures and other potential consequences)? Moreover, such projections may reflect exaggerated confidence in humanity's ability to engineer a soft landing precisely after the interim pleasantness leading up to 2.5° C concludes, but before the potentially dangerous changes kick in thereafter.

It is also important to discern whether such studies analyze the benefits or damages beyond a single sector, such as agriculture;

extrapolating from one sector to economy-wide implications is rarely warranted. Scientists and economists have, in fact, distinguished different sectors based on the shape of their "damage curves" in relation to different temperature levels. Some find that while agriculture, terrestrial ecosystems and forests may yield interim productivity gains up to some, difficult-to-estimate temperature threshold before turning negative, other sectors like coastal and marine ecosystems are more likely to experience damages even during initial temperature increases.

Finally, calls for modest and short-term goals may fail to reflect the risk of non-linear, abrupt change or potentially irreversible thresholds. The standard, linear economic method of quantifying and discounting future damages cannot really capture these largely incommensurable risks along the way.

The point here is not to presume to resolve such long-running and complex debates in these pages, but to spotlight briefly how important it is for American society to engage much more fully on the myriad dimensions of this enormously important goal-setting exercise. Currently, this is largely a debate of inside specialists, in part because the technical nature of the content creates obstacles to public participation. But the relevant work – in its scientific, economic and other variants – can and should be translated into more accessible terms so that American values and interests can be engaged, honest tradeoffs debated and choices made about how we will address the challenge of climate change. We need to broaden the debate and bring it out into the light.

Attitudinal Targets

Targets and timetables can be proposed by policy specialists and pursued with the benefit of intricate trading schemes, but ultimately they will only be implemented if there is an adequate base of public support and "will." Given this, we now turn to a relatively neglected area of goal-setting in the climate change arena, that of measurable attitudinal targets, which may be crucial precursors to the setting of emissions reductions targets and other actions on climate change.

It is not, of course, easy to ascertain with any precision what attitudinal base of support one needs in order to pave the way for a certain emissions-reduction target, since this depends centrally on the configuration of constituencies at play at a given moment. One would intuitively expect that more stringent emissions targets (i.e., those likely to impose greater costs or lifestyle adjustments) would require more stringent attitudinal goals, meaning, for example, a greater percentage of Americans saying they think climate change is a serious or very serious problem.

Pollsters typically gauge support levels for certain policy actions by seeing if they hold even if the respondent is told that significant costs would be entailed. While this presumably helps to ferret out the most committed supporters of a policy, the reliability of oral representations about a readiness to incur costs is questionable, as opposed to behavioral evidence that they actually do agree to incur it.

So what kinds of attitudinal targets could be considered, specified and measured? One target might be to increase the percentage of Americans who say, in a cross-sectional, nationally sampled poll, that climate change is a serious or very serious national problem from the current approximation of 30 percent up to 50 percent by a target date. Agreement on such a goal might suggest a broad-based, grassroots strategy rather than a leverage-point strategy targeting influentials. One might still decide that some sub-segment of the general population would be more persuadable, and therefore worthy of focus, as long as a change in that segment's attitudes would be sufficient to contribute measurably to the targeted increase in the national concern level overall.

One target might be to increase the percentage of Americans who say, in a cross-sectional, nationally sampled poll, that climate change is a serious or very serious national problem from the current approximation of 30 percent up to 50 percent by a target date.

An alternative model might be to set attitudinal targets that are reliably known to be predictive of behavior. For example, Jon Krosnick has written extensively about the "issue public" concept, which refers to that segment of the population that says an issue is personally important to them. Note that a person's answers have been shown to diverge significantly depending on whether they are asked to indicate what is important to them personally versus important to the nation as a whole. Members of the issue public are, in effect, those who get married to the issue and engage in "attitude-expressive" behaviors like writing to their elected officials and the news media, joining or donating to organizations, factoring the issue heavily into their voting, etc.

The issue public on climate change, when last measured by Krosnick in early 1998, was around 11 percent (and it had grown from 9 percent –

a statistically significant increase – during the course of the initial Kyoto Protocol debate). So one coordinating goal that those seeking to promote national emissions reductions targets might set would be to increase the climate change issue public from 11 percent to 15 percent. This may sound small, but would add over 10 million Americans to this activist segment.

Decisions on which goal to adopt (i.e., increase the proportion of Americans saying climate change is serious/very serious versus increasing the size of the issue public) are not idle. Rather, they may drive strategic choices. A strategy to target those who might be candidates for entry into issue public membership would look quite different from a broad-based strategy to raise the level of concern about the issue among the general public: its messengers, tone, arguments, and other features would be "ratcheted up" to appeal to those with a stronger set of views on the issue.

So one coordinating goal that those seeking to promote national emissions reductions targets might set would be to increase the climate change issue public from 11 percent to 15 percent. This may sound small, but would add over 10 million Americans to this activist segment.

Beyond this, there is an exceptionally wide suite of other options for identifying a specific cluster of beliefs and then doing careful pre- and post-intervention measurement to test the impact of information dissemination or other influence strategies on behalf of climate change science.

> **Energy beliefs.** One could compare what specific energy policies Americans currently support to those that would have the biggest impact on mitigating greenhouse gas emissions – and then undertake targeted communications initiatives to attempt to induce these to align more than they do today.

> **Consequences.** One could identify which of the many consequences of climate change are of greatest concern to different segments of the population through a highly textured survey and then convey specific and accurate information about that risk on a narrowcasting basis.

➤ **Geographic.** Specific attitudinal targets could be set on a geographic basis. For example, some at the Conference believe that the U.S. South could be especially pivotal in promoting national action on climate change. This is related to both partisan and religious cleavages in our society, but also adds additional cultural content. Many in the South reportedly see the North as a "know-it-all," culturally alien region, a factor that has impeded the South's assimilation of information about climate change perceived to be largely sourced in the North, or at least heavily associated with liberal Northeasterners or Californians. Southern uptake of the climate change issue would, if it is to occur, probably need to be based largely on a local rationale that is true to the cultural, religious and other traditions of the South itself. Some believe that the Katrina tragedy may prompt greater receptivity to evaluating the issue.

➤ **Certainty beliefs.** Krosnick has also investigated the substructure of beliefs on global warming and distinguished between existence beliefs (i.e., what percent of Americans believe that global warming exists), attitudes (i.e., what percentage think global warming will be, on balance, good or bad?), beliefs about human causation and efficacy, and others (see Jon Krosnick et al., "The Origins and Consequences of Democratic Citizens' Policy Agendas: A Study of Popular Concern about Global Warming," forthcoming in the journal *Climatic Change*, 2006). The variable that turns out to have the greatest impact on an individual's belief about the national seriousness of climate change is the "certainty" with which he or she holds the other beliefs (i.e., how certain are they of the existence of global warming, the role of human causation, the efficacy of remedial steps). This suggests that a potential civic engagement strategy might invest less in persuading those who don't believe global warming exists that it does exist, and relatively more in strengthening the "certainty" with which those who already believe some aspect of climate change hold that belief, perhaps through provision of accessible scientific information.

LEVERAGING THE SOCIAL SCIENCES

The facts of climate change cannot be left to speak for themselves. They must be actively communicated with the right words, in the right dosages, packaged with narrative storytelling that is based rigorously on reality, personalized with human faces, made vivid through visual imagery – and delivered by the right messengers. Doing this will require that climate change communications go from being a data-poor to a data-rich arena. Social science methods have not been adequately applied to date – and that must change, given the stakes.

Part I has already invoked the work of social scientists, including that of academic survey specialists who are well equipped to provide a more textured and ultimately actionable picture of the drivers of attitude change than standard pollsters. This needs to be extended to other scholars whose work may be relevant to society's engagement on climate change. A variety of disciplines – including psychology, linguistics, communications, sociology, political science and interdisciplinary fields like persuasion theory – have developed robust insights into the process of attitude formation, change, and persistence that could be harnessed in seeking to boost civic understanding and engagement on climate change.

For example, cognitive psychologists Daniel Kahneman and Amos Tversky produced a rich body of Nobel Prize-winning psychological work on how people make everyday judgments under conditions of uncertainty, and the simplifying shortcuts they use (see Daniel Kahneman, Paul Slovic, and Amos Tversky, eds., *Judgment Under Uncertainty: Heuristics and Biases,* Cambridge University Press, 1982). Some of these shortcuts serve people well, while others produce systematic biases and errors. Much of this work awaits extension and application to the issue of climate change and could help illuminate the following kinds of questions. How do people draw inferences when evaluating information or risks associated with climate change? What errors do they make in interpreting the probabilities of climate-related forecasts? How can optimism and other emotional or intuitive factors shape their decisions, in comparison to rational processing of the facts? What determines what people recall from their memory when making current decisions about climate change? When comparing two policy options or personal actions intended to mitigate climate change, which few features do people choose to base the decision on and why?

Much of the research on these questions also demonstrates that the way choices are framed can influence the decisions individual make. By tapping into this existing work and formulating new applied research questions, those seeking to promote civic engagement on climate change may be able to do a much better job of framing scientific and other factors for maximum understanding and motivation.

Enthusiasm has grown since we adjourned the Conference for building on our efforts to connect social and natural scientists in a problem-centered model – with climate change as a worthy case. This has spawned additional dialogues about how to promote such cross-fertilization, whether through joint panels at the annual meetings of scientific associations or deeper integration through new research programs.

So why do more social science? Perhaps the most compelling rationale is that it likely constitutes a good investment. The Conference, for example, recommended the creation of a "new overarching communications entity or project to design and execute a well-financed public education campaign on climate change science and its implications . . ." and further called for funding it with $50-100 million. Applying just a small portion of that sum to first conducting rigorous social science research should help ensure that the proposed campaign will have the desired impact on public engagement. Such research should go far beyond the routine use of qualitative focus groups or broad-brush polling and into laboratory and field experimentation to test cognitive and social psychological mechanisms. Further reinforcement for the value of such research comes, by implication, from past campaigns on climate change, which have apparently had limited impact despite considerable multi-million dollar funding in some cases.

Accordingly, a key foundational recommendation of the Conference is to undertake systematic and rigorous research to test the impact of environmental communications in all media on civic engagement, public opinion, and persuasive outcomes, and to apply the findings to inform new creative work on multi-media climate change communications (Recommendation #26).

Yale's Environmental Attitudes & Behavior Project is presently working with collaborators, including a number of the scholars who were at the Conference, to develop a research program that will apply social science theories and methods more effectively to the problem of climate change. This is not the place to sketch out the research agenda, but it is actively taking shape today, based in part on new insights and collaborations formed at the Conference. The following examples illustrate the type of research questions being formulated and considered.

Threat-Based versus Solution-Based Appeals

Environmentalists are reportedly anxious to shed their stereotype as the chicken-little, sky-is-falling, gloom-and-doom, scare-mongering skunks at the garden party. That's understandable, and it is based on a belief, echoed by many at the Conference, that a more positive, can-do approach will better motivate Americans. Better to appeal to Americans' highest hopes than their fears, right?

This surely has some validity. Yet when one hears such advice, it is always worth asking what data it is based on. Yes, environmentalists' popularity on national polls has receded a bit in recent years. But not enough research has been done to understand why. Could it have more to do with larger political realignments than an overly negative environmentalist message?

The point here is that armchair theories about what motivates people, or a general desire to shed an image, are not a solid enough foundation on which to reposition a movement or an issue. Existing theory and data should be tapped to help explain the psychological and cultural mechanisms that influence how environmentalists are perceived as messengers, as well as the persuasive impact of their use of threat-based versus solution-based appeals regarding climate change. It is important to distinguish, through controlled testing, the persuasive impact of the messengers from that of the message content – as well as interactive effects between them.

The point here is that armchair theories about what motivates people, or a general desire to shed an image, are not a solid enough foundation on which to reposition a movement or an issue.

Social scientists have conducted extensive testing on the efficacy of so-called "fear-based appeals" in health messages intended to induce public compliance with medically favored behaviors. Many such findings and methods could be extended to research on human responses to climate change messages. Should public communications about climate change emphasize the threatening consequences of inaction or the practical solutions to the problem? Or a blend of the two? If a blend, how should they be sequenced? How does this vary, if at all, based on the target audience? Some health communications research has observed that threat-based appeals can induce timely behaviors, but can also be discounted or even ignored outright if the recipient of the message is not supplied simultaneously with information on how they can effectively contend with the threat.

Crafting the optimal message requires research; it should be meticulously based on accurate scientific information about the threat to begin with and calibrated in relation to the existing concern level of the audience and their perceived ability to do something about the threat. Findings are often situational to the specific threat, the point-in-time and the specific audience, and social scientists can usefully be recruited to assist in finding answers that are of great value to communications practitioners.

Adaptation and the Loss Aversion Effect

The Conference participants debated whether adaptation messages should be featured more prominently in climate change communications. Before considering its motivational impact, the central ethical argument should first be recognized: both adaptation messages and the actual adaptation behaviors themselves have merit in that they would help vulnerable populations who will need to contend with climate change, regardless of whether causation is human-influenced or not.

But beyond this, adaptation planning could serve as a back door to a more reality-based dialogue about mitigating climate change in the first place. It would move climate change from an abstract to a concrete issue and once people were engaged in preparing for the consequences of that amount of climate change to which we are already committed due to past emissions, they would naturally begin to ask how still more climate change could be avoided (hence the pathway to discussion about reducing emissions).

This could help level the playing field so that the much-discussed economic costs of climate change regulation would be compared not to the status quo but more fairly to the costs of inaction, including the burdens of human adaptation to unabated climate change. At the Conference, there was sufficient support, qualified by some reservations, for a recommendation calling for increased emphasis on adaptation and preparedness for climate change (Recommendation #22).

Given that this remains an area of debate and the recommendation was based largely on intuition, we can turn to the social sciences to do rigorous testing about how people might actually respond to adaptation-oriented messages and behaviors. Kahneman et al., for example, observed a robust phenomenon they dubbed "loss aversion," which showed how individuals' preferences can actually reverse based on their perceived reference point, in violation of basic tenets of expected utility theory.

Let's start with a simple example whereby the "loss aversion" principle becomes manifested in an "endowment effect." Let's say I give you a coffee mug worth $10. I then ask you how much someone would have to pay you to relinquish it. It turns out that statistically significant numbers of people in this situation ask for more to relinquish the mug they already possess (say $12), than they are willing to pay to acquire that same mug if they didn't already have it (say $7). This valuation asymmetry is based on their reference point (i.e., whether they possess the mug or don't) and it defies standard economic analysis, in which the mug would be valued equivalently regardless of whether one possesses it or not at that moment. How people set their reference point (which is often but not always their perceived status quo) and what can induce a shift in it, then becomes a pivotal issue in explaining the decisions they make.

Extending this asymmetry to a more complex case, people who regard themselves as having already lost something (i.e., as being in a "domain of losses" relative to their reference point) will often choose a risky option over a sure gain, even if the probability-adjusted payout of the risky choice is lower than the sure gain. What draws them is the probabilistic chance that the risky choice will allow them to restore their losses all the way back to their reference point, typically the status quo ante. By contrast, those who perceive that they are positioned ahead of their reference point and therefore in a "domain of gains" will typically choose a sure gain over a risky choice offering a higher probability-adjusted payout (i.e., they make a risk-averse choice).

So what does all this have to do with adaptation? If Americans perceive their reference point to be the status quo of a fairly stable, hospitable climate, these findings could be interpreted to posit, subject to testing, that they would be less likely to invest in costly emissions reductions efforts with a higher probability-adjusted payout in the future than to take what they regard as a sure gain (i.e., keep the money they would have otherwise invested in emissions reductions). If, on the other hand, they can be induced to recognize that we are already in a domain of losses by virtue of past emissions and the adaptation "overhang" they have created, then Americans may be more inclined to invest in more intensive emissions reductions efforts that hold out the chance of stabilizing greenhouse gases at a non-dangerous level in the atmosphere. Without testing, we cannot know whether adaptation messages, or actual engagement in adaptation planning, would induce this kind of reference point shift and prompt Americans to favor more stringent or more "urgent" emissions reduction policies, but it bears rigorous investigation.

This exploratory sketch is not meant to suggest that this or any other body of cognitive research can be applied to climate change in a paint-by-numbers fashion. Extending and applying social science work requires the caution, rigor and expertise of social scientists, working in tandem with real-world practitioners. But the point is that we have not begun to scratch the surface of what such investigations could yield in terms of promoting civic engagement and action on climate change, so there is much promising work ahead.

Dynamic Responses and Canceling Out

Given the partisanship and controversy that has afflicted the climate change issue, it is important to better test and understand how individuals respond to being cross-pressured by opposing or otherwise varied arguments. There is little question that Americans are somewhat confused about environmental issues. For example, a 2005 Yale Environmental Poll found that 53 percent of Americans agree with the statement: "There is so much information and disagreement in the media that I don't know who to believe about what is best for the environment." Since most climate change policies do entail costs to some in society, any initial success that a concerted communications campaign on climate change experiences is likely to elicit counter-advertising as to why the proposed actions should not be taken. As a result, the longer-term success of any climate change communications campaign will likely depend on the extent to which the focal messages of the campaign are able to survive counterattack.

Rigorous pre-testing can reveal the kinds of argument that are most robust. Social science can reveal how arguments and counter-arguments cancel one another out in the minds of the public, depending on their relative volume, quality and other comparative attributes. This should be done not only upfront before a communications campaign is launched, but also in iterative updates that allow recalibration of messages based on unfolding evidence about the audience's response to cross-pressures.

Issue Cycles

How can climate change emerge amidst the severe competition for space on the national agenda? We know that it ranks relatively low on the public ranking of issues of concern, but don't yet know enough about the factors that could cause climate change to move ahead of other issues. We tend to believe that media coverage is a big factor, but social science evidence for the media's "agenda-priming" capability is mixed and, in fact, a significant body of research has found that media coverage has "minimal effects" on public opinion. This may be, in part, because those in an audience whose opinions prove to be most susceptible to media influence – i.e., those whose concern is most appreciably boosted by an issue communication – tend to be the least informed on an issue. More importantly, their concern level, in turn, tends to be relatively unstable, subsiding just as quickly as it spiked (see Richard E. Petty and Jon A. Krosnick, *Attitude Strength: Antecedents or Consequences*, Lawrence Erlbaum Associates, May 1995). So if the goal is to build a cumulative base of public support for action over some period, reliance on media-based messages alone may be unwise.

Findings like these, if robust across multiple studies, can significantly reorient one's investments in how to communicate about an issue like climate change. Channels that are perceived to be high impact may prove less so, once the stability of the achieved attitude change over time is evaluated. Climate change is at a stage in its maturation as an issue where it requires the most sophisticated possible research about public attitudes, motivation and behavior. Armchair speculation is not sufficient.

A number of political scientists have portrayed the dynamics of how issues cycle through the national agenda. Anthony Downs described a five-stage cycle, with the spike in "issue-attention" occurring in the second stage when a dramatic event brings a particular issue to the public's attention. This occurred for climate change in 1988 in the United States, during the worst drought in 50 years and an exceptionally hot summer – punctuated by NASA scientist James Hansen's testimony to Congress. Unfortunately, later stages of Downs' cycle also appear to have been borne out, as the costs and threats associated with solving a problem diminish the public's ardor to undertake remedial action – and finally the public succumbs to relative boredom if not complete obliviousness about the issue that had previously gripped it (see Anthony Downs, *Political Theory and Public Choice*, Edward Elgar Publications, July 1998).

More recently, political scientist Frank Baumgartner, a participant at our Conference, has borrowed from biology's punctuated equilibrium theory to describe the episodic intensification of public attention and action on issues like climate change (see Robert Repetto, Editor, *Punctuated Equilibrium and the Dynamics of U.S. Environmental Policy*, Yale University Press, May 2006). This is driven by a set of mutually reinforcing factors, many of them resistant to intentional orchestration, that must be better understood if we are to fashion a successful model for civic engagement on climate change.

Part II

Diagnoses and Recommendations

INTRODUCTION

Part II of this report describes each group's answers to their two-part charge:

1. Diagnose how your domain may have contributed to the gap between climate science and policy and action (due to such factors as occupational identities, norms, practices, incentive systems and others); and

2. Develop ideas and initiatives to help close the gap, both through action steps within your domain and new or enhanced cross-domain collaborations.

This overarching charge was customized further to each domain by the supplemental questions that open each section below. Time did not permit full answers to these big questions, but we hope that by including them in this report, readers will be inspired to attempt their own answers and to share those with us at our interactive website: *http://environment.yale.edu/climate*. This website is intended to become the hub for tracking, and attracting participation in, implementation of the 39 action recommendations.

The results reported below reflect core input from those representing each domain, who initially met in separate working groups. But they also draw on insights from those in other domains, who were subsequently mixed in to refine, extend and reality-test the initial ideas, as well as to add their own new ones. We did not seek to attain consensus, but rather to draw out and report on the full range of views. Therefore, once again, the reader is reminded not to construe individual or collective sign-off by the Conference participants on any specific points or recommendations.

Science

QUESTIONS

Should scientists take more forceful roles in conveying climate change science?

In what ways do scientists limit their roles deliberately due to occupational norms, identity, and incentives?

Should such constraints be modified in light of the special features of the climate change problem itself (e.g., irreversibility, encompassing scope) or persistent indicators of public and policy-maker confusion on the issue?

Why hasn't past outreach by scientists on climate change had more impact in promoting action commensurate with the problem – for example, their communication of findings of the Intergovernmental Panel on Climate Change (IPCC) and the National Academy of Sciences?

What new arrangements or other innovations are needed to ensure that good science is injected into public discourse and the policy process?

DIAGNOSIS

> **Word choice.** Scientists often use words in ways that vary from public usage. As a result, scientific findings are not framed in a way that is accessible to non-scientific decision-makers and the general public. Some examples:

  - "Positive feedbacks" are a major concern in climate science because they reflect exacerbation of the original warming caused by greenhouse gases, but to the public, "positive" sounds good. A phrase like "vicious cycle" would be more understandable.

  - "Radiation" is used in climate science to refer to heat dynamics, but to the layperson this term connotes cancer treatment, nuclear weapons, or Chernobyl, the world's worst nuclear accident.

  - Discussions of confidence levels and probabilities perpetuate a sense of controversy, even in areas where the scientific consensus is quite strong. On the positive side, the IPCC statement that most of the observed warming of the past 50 years is due to human impact was viewed by many as an example of clear communication.

➤ **Puzzles, not consensus.** Scientists' predilection is to emphasize puzzles, uncertainties, caveats and details that the public cannot absorb, rather than to adhere to standard principles of communication that emphasize repetition of known, core points.

- The length and complexity of some scientific reports is a big barrier. For example, the reports of the IPCC, including its summaries, are scientifically impeccable but too lengthy and complex for most decision-makers or consumers in the general public – they need the ten-page version.

➤ **Conservatism.** Scientists are fundamentally conservative and risk averse when it comes to engagement beyond their standard peer group audiences. They are typically hesitant to initiate or even be drawn into efforts to communicate to policy-makers, the media, or the general public, often out of concern that their work will not be communicated accurately. Given this concern, scientists are especially reluctant to get out ahead of society and articulate the need for urgent or drastic steps.

- A substantial part of scientists' conservatism stems from the culture and norms of their profession, as reflected in the lack of academic incentives to communicate science to the general public. Most focus, instead, on communicating their work to other trained scientists. They are discouraged from diverting precious research and career-building time to outreach activities. And many are sensitive to risks to their reputations from being seen as too eager to gain public attention for their research or to take a position on a contentious matter of public policy. This sensitivity is increased further by the attendant risk of magnifying any methodological or other scientific errors they make in front of a larger audience, with greater risk of backlash and embarrassment.

- Even those scientists who do attempt to overcome this incentive structure and project their findings to a broader audience frequently lack the training to do so effectively. There is a lamentable lack of early training for young scientists in communicating to a general audience.

- Scientists who work in disciplines or sub-disciplines that are especially prone to flux express extra reticence to speak out. In such cases, it can be difficult to translate qualified or tentative findings to broader audiences or to make them relevant to the public – say, at the ecosystem impact level – where they can inform action.

- Scientists' affinity for expressing their findings in written form can be a problem, given the public's increasing move toward visual media.

➢ **Lack of rewards for interdisciplinary work.** The scientific reward structure in research universities and institutes encourages depth and specialization, not interdisciplinary work. The research agenda is set by individual scientists pursuing their own curiosity, interests and career needs, not by broader public or policy needs.

- Because scientific uncertainty tends to be greatest amidst competing theories at the cutting edge that gain notoriety, the public may think such uncertainty is also characteristic of core science, including the uncontroversial parts of climate science.

- The IPCC is an inspiring example of inter-disciplinary and collaborative work, but it draws essentially on volunteer time, which many scientists with pressing academic commitments cannot afford to give.

- A number of climate change research areas of enormous societal importance have not attracted the critical mass of scientists or funding necessary.

  - Research on climate change impacts is, in the view of some, in a deplorable state, especially on the local scale, which is critical to increasing public engagement and policy action.

  - Other understudied areas include the ongoing release of methane from melting permafrost, which could have enormous climate change impacts, but has not yet attracted a critical mass of scholars or funding.

RECOMMENDED ACTIONS

> **Recommendation #1:** *Create a new "bridging institution" to actively seek out key business, religious, political, and civic leaders and the media and deliver to them independent, reliable and credible scientific information about climate change (including natural and economic sciences).*

- ➤ **Trusted voice.** This institution would serve as an independent, forceful, trusted voice that articulates the science of climate change. Its team would attempt to remain entirely separate from vested interests or advocacy groups engaged in the climate change arena. It would similarly seek to avoid the perception that it is an advocacy group itself, despite inevitable efforts to portray it as such. It would do this by strictly guarding its objectivity and communicating only the most unimpeachable, peer-reviewed science.

- ➤ **Top scientists.** Top scientists would commit in the founding phase to seek audiences in an organized way through this new institution.

- ➤ **Proactive.** The group would be highly proactive and take its "show" on the road: to editorial boards, managing editors, congressional staffers and members, governors, CEOs, mayors, university presidents, CEOs of media organizations, network anchors, columnists, and TV producers. It would take a retail, not wholesale, approach to the task and orchestrate a series of personal, often local, connections.

- ➤ **Responsive.** In addition to its proactive work, this institution would be available to respond to incoming inquiries on climate change science from the public, the media and all organizations with an interest in independent information to assist them in understanding or addressing climate change. As such, it would serve as a one-stop shop. Given the potentially large volume of inquiries, special attention would be given to avoiding bottlenecks and maximizing response time, including an efficient information architecture, online and phone access, searchable databases, multi-media resources, outstanding cross-referenced expert guides and other elements.

The Bridging Institution's Mandate

- Educate institutional leaders and the general public about the basics of climate change and methods by which consensus has arisen.

- Disseminate new findings much more quickly than is possible through peer-reviewed journals.

- Conduct rapid response to invalidate myths or other disinformation.

- Clarify the climate change dimension of topical events (e.g., Hurricane Katrina).

- Serve as a support network for other scientists not necessarily associated with the institution who speak out on climate change.

- Conduct surveys of scientists on climate change issues.

- Produce consensus statements.

- Develop an information dissemination plan using the most effective communication vehicles, including websites, press releases, news feeds, weather channel information, etc.

- Encourage media outreach by scientists and the capacity-building required to succeed, including training scientists to speak in language that is understandable to different audiences. In particular, provide media and communications training, (e.g., by building on the success of such programs as the Aldo Leopold Leadership Program).

> **Models.** Several existing institutions have been cited as either models (e.g., COMPASS) or potential homes (e.g., AAAS) to which a sub-unit tasked with this mandate could be appended. COMPASS stands for Communication Partnership for Science and the Sea, and was launched in October 1999 to "increase the use of scientific information in marine conservation policy and practice by making academic science less fragmented, and more applicable, available, and understandable to a wide audience." AAAS stands for the American Association for the Advancement of Science and is an international non-profit organization

dedicated to advancing science around the world by serving as an educator, leader and professional association. It publishes the prestigious journal *Science*.

➢ **Anticipating the task.** The institution would help scientists anticipate the communications/outreach task earlier in the process of framing their research questions, not as an add-on.

➢ **Dominated by scientists.** The institution would be dominated by scientists, but would draw in and leverage talents from other domains. It would enlist other credible, non-scientific opinion leaders, business leaders, and other respected individuals to communicate climate science.

➢ **Continuously updated.** Details of the content of what the Institution would communicate would be continuously updated as new findings arose. However, there would be some important standard elements:

- Discipline in repeating core elements of the scientific consensus on climate change.

- Pointing out the limits of emergent knowledge (e.g., combating simplistic thinking about sequestration as a cure-all for greenhouse gas emissions).

- Exploring and designing metaphors for communicating about the global environment (e.g., a global park).

- Shifting the burden of proof so that public expectations of certainty would be conditioned over time to give way to a risk management paradigm. Some have urged that we should go further, beyond the risk management paradigm, which raises its own contentious problems of balancing hard-to-quantify risks and benefits, and toward a precautionary paradigm, which was a crucial underpinning of eventual action on phasing out CFCs that deplete the ozone layer and would be better suited to motivating significant action on climate change.

➢ **Strategic dialogues.** The institution would invest in strategic dialogues to acquire a better understanding of why or why not key leaders in different segments of the public embrace climate change as a major issue, and what kinds of scientific information on climate change each would want or need.

➤ **Reframe the focus.** Based on these audience and constituency understandings, the institution would reframe the focus of climate change communications or the tactical language used. It would pre-test specific word choices to assess how audiences hear them, and be especially careful to anticipate colloquial interpretation of scientific terms.

➤ **New communication tools.** It would develop new communication tools to disseminate information about local impacts and other climate change information to the general public (e.g., a webpage for impacts with a map/zip code function so that the general public could easily access information on how climate change could affect them).

➤ **Climate Index.** The institution could create a Climate Index that integrates various indicators of climate change into an understandable form (e.g., temperature rise, heat stress, intense precipitation events, sea level). Enlist scientific expertise to make it credible, but also especially amenable to localization to the extent that the indicators permit.

➤ **Overcome reticence.** The institution would also be charged with seeking to address, and overcome, the factors that induce scientists' reticence in communicating, by modeling more outspokenness, but also influencing leaders of scientific, governmental and university institutions to change norms, internal culture, and incentives.

➤ **Harness existing NGO mechanisms.** Existing NGOs should not be underestimated as highly leveraged points for disseminating climate change science, especially given that so few NGOs currently have resident scientific expertise. Scientists could individually approach NGOs to serve on committees or boards, in ways that are consistent with their objectivity, but also harness existing relationships and communications mechanisms the NGOs have built. The new institution should be kept entirely independent of advocacy or non-scientific organizations, although the latter could be users of its output.

➤ **Mentoring.** The institution would organize mentoring efforts by which senior scientists who have successfully navigated the communication of cutting-edge science could help younger scientists do so more effectively.

➢ **Obligating outreach.** Help promote scientists' readiness to talk to the media by making outreach obligatory among those receiving grants from the National Science Foundation, NASA, the National Academy of Sciences and other institutions.

➢ **Support training.** Support institutional capacity for media and outreach training. The institution should provide training and augment the capacity of other institutions to provide this, specifically in relation to climate change. The institution should provide a menu of options for its own training, such as two-to-three day programs or two-week summer programs. These programs should be led by the giants in the field. The institution should also reach out to the AAAS about its media training sessions that few attend and those at other universities (e.g., fellowships and courses at Scripps Institute, Woods Hole, Lamont Doherty, MIT, Stanford). How can these be expanded and how can others be recruited to attend?

➢ **Content of media training**. Media training courses for scientists should include how to testify, how to write Op-Eds, how to anticipate how words will be reported (e.g., relative emphasis on certainties and uncertainties), how to cover different aspects of science, and how journalists work.

  • *Heroes.* In particular, help journalists identify stories that connect science to culture (e.g., scientific heroes doing work on climate change).

  • *Training.* Provide training, above all, for scientists to talk in a comprehensible way. Journalists are not inclined to train scientists or coax clear language out of them, but to take their subject as they find it. So the burden is on the scientists, or others who want scientists to succeed, to communicate more effectively. Help identify words that scientists can use to portray the climate change issue in a more compelling fashion to journalists and the general public (e.g., climate disruption instead of climate change). Moreover, scientists must be trained not just to get facts out, but how to introduce and sustain them in the face of a polemical response. Make sure this is covered in media training, especially given the rise in contentious media formats that value debate above all else.

- *Personalize the story.* Highlight the personal dimension of the climate change story, even at the highest levels of power (e.g., how the relationship between President George W. Bush and UK Prime Minister Tony Blair on the climate change issue has taken on added interest following their Iraq War alliance).

- *Narrative Drive.* Identify the "gee whiz" mysteries in climate change to provoke audience interest and engagement. This could exacerbate the problem of highlighting uncertainties more than the large zone of scientific consensus. But if handled well – as it was in the TV series *Strange Days on Planet Earth,* for example – it can also draw the audience into a more active stance on the issue.

➢ **University experts lists.** Leverage existing assets like university "experts lists." Do they all have climate change represented fully? Are all relevant scientists cross-referenced on all climate-related topics, including extreme weather events, droughts and other topical impact stories?

➢ **First step toward establishing the institution.** Convene a workshop of possible funders, scientists, and other key players and users to benchmark existing institutions with a similar mandate and to develop a blueprint of what the new institution (or a new unit of an existing institution, like the American Association for the Advancement of Science or The Science Media Centre in London) might look like.

Recommendation #2: *Reorient research priorities on climate change to be more responsive to society's information and decision-making needs, including greater emphasis on impacts, local consequences, timing, non-linear risks, adaptation, and solutions.*

➢ **Broaden the circle.** Create mechanisms to broaden the circle of influencers and decision-makers determining the research agenda beyond scientists themselves.

➢ **Focus more research on:**

- Climate change impacts, especially at the local level;

- Non-linear consequences and feedbacks that could inform society's level of urgency on climate change, such as methane releases from permafrost melting or reduced surface reflectivity from polar ice melting;

- Adaptation and preparedness, extending from the sciences into applied technical and engineering work;

- Solutions (both mitigation and adaptation);

- Integrated visions of alternative futures that are scientifically coherent and could inform public understanding of the implications of alternative societal actions;

- Establishing scientifically calibrated temperature targets and endpoints in light of impacts research, and backing up from these targets to actionable prescriptions;

- Applied social science that can inform how natural scientific findings are communicated to society.

Recommendation #3: *Strengthen citizen-science initiatives on climate change so as to build greater public engagement with the conduct of climate change science.*

➢ **Closer engagement.** This should produce closer engagement between scientists and society, not just in terms of disseminating scientific results and broadening input into the research agenda, but specifically by engaging the public in the research process itself. This initiative should begin by assembling and synthesizing the results of the many citizen climate change efforts now underway. It should then encourage scientists to collaborate on developing best practices guidance or another quality control mechanism for citizen science, so that these efforts are considered scientifically (and not just politically) legitimate.

➢ **Technical example of citizen-science: distributed computing.** Members of the general public have been contributing the idle processing capacity of their personal computers – through the Internet – to a massive set of distributed computing experiments organized at *www.climateprediction.net.* These experiments require consent by the users and afford them a sense of involvement in the projects, as well as access to the findings. The scientists, meanwhile, gain access to much more computing power than they would otherwise be able to harness. This innovative work has produced genuinely important – and, in some cases, troubling – findings. In a study published by Oxford climate modeler David Stainforth in the January 27, 2005 issue of the scientific journal *Nature*, a model that ran on 26,000 idle computers found that six so-called "perturbed parameters" could interact in a non-linear fashion to produce higher climate sensitivity to greenhouse gases than had been found in any previous study – up to 19.8° Fahrenheit (or 3.6° higher than any previous study). This is not to say this high sensitivity is likely (they were silent on probability), but such models help to establish a range that extends out to the worst case.

➢ **Non-technical example of citizen-science: bird counts.** A leading non-technical example of citizen-science to build on is the Audubon Society's Christmas Bird Count database, for which 106 years of records submitted largely by amateur birdwatchers have been captured – and are now computerized. Public participation has increased steadily over the years.

Over the past 40 years, there have been 1,000 to 2,000 Christmas Bird Counts per year with up to 200 species per location. Numbers of each species are counted, so there is good information on changes in abundance, not just presence versus absence.

Many birds are considered "charismatic species," and as such their familiarity to many Americans makes them ideal for communicating the effects of climate change.

In fact, the Audubon data from the mid-1960s shows that many species of birds are wintering farther north, providing additional evidence that the warming at northerly latitudes is influencing the behavior of species in relation to their habitats. The Audubon data is robust, representing a wide variety of species with many ecological niches. Audubon researchers are now aiming to undertake a verification of the finding about northern range extensions by analyzing all the species on the Christmas Bird Count over the 40 year period (about 400-450 species with sufficient sample sizes). They will also undertake selective lookbacks earlier in the century for key indicator and representative species.

Recommendation #4: *Identify and execute feasible, high-level actions that could modify the financial and reward structures within academia most responsible for inhibiting: a) interdisciplinary and problem-oriented research on large-scale, urgent issues like climate change; and b) faculty and PhD student engagement in public communication, policy-making and other public service arenas. Recruit key influencers to meet with university presidents, university funders, and other influencers in furtherance of this objective.*

➤ **Exert pressure to change incentive structures.** These incentives have a profound influence on constraining interdisciplinary research as well as public outreach by scientists. While it is generally accepted that it is difficult to change academic institutions, the significance of the stakes makes high-level entreaties to accomplish changes worthwhile.

➤ **Enlist university presidents.** Attempts should therefore be made to enlist university presidents, perhaps through their associations and journals, and other informal peer-to-peer dialogues, to conduct significant re-evaluations of how their institutions discourage outreach at present, and how this could be changed. Some also look to foundations and other funders to expand the nascent outreach components required for research grants.

➤ **Leverage foundation support.** Foundations and other philanthropic organizations are widely recognized as vital funders of the university enterprise. As such, they could exercise considerable influence in driving changes in incentive structures, both directly by reaching out to key university officials and by attaching requirements to their grants requiring, for example, significant public communication and outreach work by the grantees. They could similarly put a greater priority on funding the kind of interdisciplinary research that is so critical to climate change science.

➤ **Reduce risks to faculty.** Identify ways to reduce or eliminate career penalties and risks to university faculty and other researchers from communicating their work.

- Protect them from overt intimidation by those who would prefer that they refrain from informing contentious debates with research findings.

- Also seek to counter the "gotcha" risk that breeds norms of excessive caution in scientific academia; some feel that the risks of being caught in a small mistake are typically exaggerated in relation to the importance of getting the general principles right.

Recommendation #5: *Identify mechanisms to preserve and advance the integrity of the publicly-funded scientific research enterprise, especially on climate change. Shine a public spotlight on the process by which the federal science agenda is developed and funding choices are made.*

Recommendation #6: *Convene one or more dialogues free of economic and political compromises to undertake a fundamental redefinition of the climate change challenge in light of its urgency.*

➤ **Delineated issues.** Define a sharper outline of the major issues and urgencies associated with climate change.

➤ **Kyoto limitations.** Clarify that policy instruments such as the Kyoto Protocol, while a useful first step, are ultimately insufficient, given their model of constant emissions based on recent baselines rather than substantial reductions converging on zero net emissions in the future.

➤ **Scientific credibility.** Harness scientific credibility in exposing the scale of the problem.

➤ **Public interest.** Redefine the imperative of governmental action that more fully reflects public interest, rather than special-interest constituencies.

News Media

QUESTIONS

How have the frequency, context, tone and placement of news coverage on climate change science shaped policy-maker and public responses?

Is the media's resident scientific expertise a limitation, and should it be supplemented by better access to impartial scientists or intermediaries?

How have journalistic norms, such as balance and source identification, affected coverage, and should they be modified or administered differently?

What ownership and market pressures constrain climate science coverage, whether through compression of formats, blurring of the news/entertainment line, "breaking news" dynamics, "imitative cascades" of media attention, or advertiser influence?

DIAGNOSIS

➢ **Gatekeepers not convinced.** News gatekeepers such as news editors and directors have not considered climate change a priority. Journalists are often discouraged by their editors from reporting on the issue. Top editors at the major U.S. papers are particularly important because they set the agenda for the rest of the U.S. media, and this group has yet to decide whether climate change is a problem. Some vigorously contend that the media *reflect* rather than *set* the agenda – and therefore cannot be expected to take a leadership role in increasing climate change's prominence on the national agenda. Debate over the relative autonomy and influence of the news media is on-going.

➢ **Gap in science education.** Editors and journalists lack literacy in science generally and in climate science specifically. Similarly, the general public itself lacks the scientific education required to understand the implications of the issue. To the extent that news media reflect rather than shape society, their approach to climate change currently mirrors the gap in science education within society.

➢ **Disinformation campaigns.** Editors and journalists appear to have been influenced by disinformation campaigns on climate change, which has further exacerbated the scientific education gap since a lack of training makes it more difficult to distinguish rigorous science from manipulated or selective representations of the science.

> **A difficult story to tell.** Rarely is there an anecdotal lead in a climate change story to drive the narrative and promote a sense of personal relevance, whether a likely victim of potential climate change impacts, an entrepreneur with a solution or a scientist-hero. Instead of human interest pegs, climate change stories tend to contain complex and abstract scientific information and follow a numbing structure: some event occurs (e.g., collapse of an ice shelf), the basic climate change science is spelled out, alternative explanations are offered, and the IPCC or some other authoritative source is cited, implying that more research is needed. These stories are sufficiently similar that the reader has little sense that the science has advanced.

> **Long-term issue.** Climate change is perceived by many as a long, slow-moving process with consequences only far in the future. It is not considered today's story. The press does not currently have the tools or machinery for studying and reporting on such long-term changes. Journalists are inclined to write stories that have immediacy and obvious urgency, and so far the abrupt climate change scenarios positing near to mid-term surprises have not broken through sufficiently to change the perceived character of the issue as a slowly unfolding one.

- Projected mean temperature changes of one or two degrees sound pleasant to some, and understanding of the negative environmental consequences of these changes is limited.

- The international dimensions of the climate change story appear to be of limited interest among the American public.

- The climate change story is rarely told with a villain; in fact, to the extent that the public correctly perceives that climate change is connected to energy use, they may recognize their broad complicity, which limits the conflict narrative further.

> **Career incentives (and penalties).** Coverage of climate change and other complex scientific issues is not perceived as a path to career advancement for journalists. Wars, the White House, and other high-profile stories offer much greater opportunity for front-page or lead-off placements.

> **Economic pressures.** The mainstream news media are increasingly owned by large consolidated companies with a short-term earnings focus and little or no commitment to civic journalism if it entails a risk to profits. Relative to other more easily hyped stories, they are inclined to refrain from covering stories like climate change because it is unlikely to attract a comparable number of viewers and readers. The mainstream news media also, according to some, resist coverage of issues like climate change because of actual or anticipated pressure from the corporate advertisers or from politicians or other influencers opposed to action on the issue.

> **Fear of attack.** Related to, but separate from, the economic pressures cited above, some mainstream journalists are reportedly inhibited by fear of professional attacks from political partisans if they do not report a scientifically discredited or out-lier perspective that is favored by such partisans. Evolution and the careful balancing using the Intelligent Design perspective constitute an instructive example.

> **Few national political champions.** The political pages of newspapers are not devoting much coverage to climate change, in part because there have been few national champions on the issue, with some notable exceptions. Without vocal champions, the press is more likely simply to mirror the lower priority that society today places on addressing climate change.

> **Not enough news about solutions.** The news media need to have access to more newsworthy stories about solutions to the climate change problem. In their absence, the audience may tune out on further illustrations of the seriousness of the crisis. One of the accurately portrayed dimensions of the issue is that even if mitigation actions are undertaken now, we are already committed to significant climate change based on past emissions, a reality that can engender futility in the audience.

> **Insufficient clarity about goals among issue experts.** Journalists covering climate change interview experts who often do not know

what decision they're trying to influence, or are not sufficiently clear in communicating it. Reporters have an affinity for lines of debate and conflict among purposeful entities and personalities. Those seeking greater action on climate change may be seeking everything from policy changes to personal behavior changes in energy conservation. These diffuse objectives may hinder coverage.

> **Fragmentation of viewership.** Audiences have access to increasingly narrow sources of news via the Internet as well as niche program and station options on cable TV. Some believe audiences tend to seek out news that reinforces, rather than challenges, their views; but others believe the data does not support this view and that purportedly liberal shows have evenly split listeners between conservatives and liberals. Other demographic attributes such as educational level may determine choices more than ideology.

> **Print versus broadcast.** Climate change scientists tend to communicate through the print medium and the story arguably lends itself to the nuance and context available via print. But audiences increasingly gravitate to broadcast media, where the climate story has not – to date – been told as well.

> **Cutting across beats.** The climate issue cannot be adequately covered by one beat, but instead cuts from the political beat to the business beat to the science beat. Given the need for a whole cadre of journalists to be informed on the issue, even within a single news organization, the communications burden is greater. This, again, reinforces the importance of efficiently getting to the gatekeeper presiding over the full organization.

> **Catch-22.** Scientists face disincentives to reach out to the media and need to be trained to do so effectively. Journalists are unwilling to become their tutors, seeing it as a compromise of their objectivity. So scientists need to look elsewhere for training and intermediaries, such as PR professionals, at some risk to their credibility. Perhaps scientific organizations or committees, not individuals, are best situated to enlist the services of PR professionals, as they did in garnering successful coverage of the Arctic Impact Assessment. However, dozens of collective scientific statements on climate change have garnered limited coverage, perhaps because they appear bureaucratic and consensus-driven rather than offering the lines of debate required for a news story.

> **United States vs. the rest of the world.** According to some, the U.S. news media vary from media abroad, to the detriment of accurate climate change coverage in this country. The BBC in the United Kingdom is cited as a news institution that has, in "benevolent dictator" fashion, devoted much less coverage to contrarian voices on climate change of dubious scientific credibility – and that has, as a result, helped to create a stronger societal consensus on the urgency of addressing the issue. Some note that scientists who speak out in the U.S. media on a contentious issue like climate change risk character assassination in return for almost no professional upside. In some developing countries, by contrast, it is expected that scientists will connect to the news media as a way to influence policy in accordance with scientific findings, so the professional risks are reduced.

> **Lack of support and incentives.** Academic institutions do not support outreach to news organizations by scientists. The rewards and incentives for doing outreach are simply not present and outreach is looked down upon as selling out by peers.

> **Lack of science communications training.** Scientists do not receive training in how to communicate outside of academia. Skills such as interviewing and writing Op-Eds can be taught and learned; however, they typically are not.

> **Objectivity.** Objectivity is one of the core values of conventional journalism. Journalists strive to be objective by telling both sides of the story. When reporting on climate change, journalists often quote contrarians to introduce "balance" to the story, which ultimately misrepresents the scientific consensus. Some insist that dissenters should be fully covered as an important part of the story, provided their funding or other influences can be disclosed and reported, and that they have something newsworthy and timely to add. In particular, industry scientists should not – in this view – be prematurely dismissed as vested interests; in many cases, they are thoughtful scientists who care about the ecological impacts of their products.

> **The importance of keeping scientists at arms length.** Journalists are keen as a group to know more about the scientific facts and how to report on them. Yet journalists are also wary of being seen as conspiring with scientists to get their story in the media. This would be not considered objective reporting, but rather a potential conflict of interest, or even an unacceptable crossover into advocacy.

➤ **Lack of resources.** Even those journalists who may want to know more about science and how best to report it rarely have the time or institutional support or funding to do so. The Metcalf Institute, among others, addresses this issue by holding workshops and training sessions for journalists, but there is a need to augment such efforts.

➤ **Tendency to rely on free media only (i.e., news media).** Some emphasize that it is important for those seeking to raise awareness and promote action on climate change not to put all their eggs in the news media basket. The temptation by those with limited, non-profit budgets is to do guerilla marketing that aims to secure the so-called "free media" that comes from getting news coverage for your statements or actions. But other vehicles for agenda-setting and issue communication should be harnessed, including underwriting of special projects, paid advertising, etc.

RECOMMENDED ACTIONS

> **Recommendation #7:** *Educate the gatekeepers (i.e., editors). In order to improve the communication of climate science in the news media, foster a series of visits and conferences whereby respected journalists and editors informed on climate change can speak to their peer editors. The objective is to have those who can credibly talk about story ideas and craft reach out to their peers about how to cover the climate change issue with appropriate urgency, context, and journalistic integrity.*

➤ **Orchestrate roadshows.** To ensure maximum exposure to these events for gatekeepers, it will be necessary to take the show on the road. Presentations should be made in the newsroom, with free lunch provided. Editors will not go elsewhere, as they lack the time, resources, and inclination.

➤ **Focus on journalists and editors, not scientists, as messengers.** The media world is relatively insular. The most credible messengers to news editors and directors are their peers, either other editors or respected journalists in the field. Scientists are considered an interest group by some in the news media. If editors are seen coaching scientists, that would be viewed as a form of advocacy.

> **Target other important gatekeeper constituencies.** Publishers should also be addressed given their role in answering to advertiser pressures.

> **Spotlight historical examples of news media missing a big story.** Identify and spotlight historical examples where newspapers have apologized to readers after the fact for failing to adequately investigate a story (e.g., the civil rights movement). Raise the question: Is climate change today such a story? Appeal to the historical legacy of the gatekeepers.

> **Identify and disseminate compelling climate change stories – and axes of conflict – so as to better engage audience interest.** Some believe that a more pronounced effort should be made to spotlight bad actors on the climate change issue, i.e., those vested interests who may be muddying the science or otherwise impeding an accurate public understanding of the issue. These stories contain elements of conflict and drama and could be more effectively highlighted in mainstream programs such as 60 Minutes and others. Investigative reporting should be expanded on who is funding scientific work across the board, so that agendas can be disclosed and the public can have the context it needs.

> **Get climate change into other newspaper sections.** Seek to move climate change from the science or environment pages into the other sections whenever possible (e.g., foreign news, political news, even feature coverage of personalities associated with the issue).

> **Get climate change on the agenda of news media associations, conferences and other high-volume gathering points.** One example is the American Society of News Editors Annual Conference. Similar sessions could be added to the broadcast journalist's conference.

> **Recommendation #8:** *Enhance the scientific competence of journalists.*

Journalists often lack scientific understanding and training in how to communicate science in the news. The following efforts could be undertaken to increase journalists' scientific knowledge:

> **Recruit scientifically savvy journalists.** News organizations should consider recruiting more staff with science backgrounds,

including from programs where journalism students are required or encouraged to gain scientific training. One standout example, and valuable recruiting ground, is the Boston University science journalism program.

> **Provide scientific reporting training.** Journalists are keen to learn more about science, but typically lack the time or money to do so. Additional training opportunities should be provided, such as fellowships to scientific institutions. One model that was mentioned is the Yale Law School fellowship for journalists. The Yale School of Forestry & Environmental Studies and other educational and scientific institutions should provide such fellowships to train journalists to report science and climate change. Funds need to be made available to journalists to take up these opportunities, as well as to attend events where they are able to meet and engage with scientists.

> **Provide information clearinghouse for scientific resources.** Establish an online clearinghouse where journalists can go for scientific resources to aid them in their story research on climate-change related topics.

> **Assist journalists in localizing the story.** Provide local journalists more information to use in localizing the climate change issue whenever possible, in terms of identifying local impacts but also finding local college scientists who can speak to local newspapers. Trust is a local currency.

> **Leverage journalism school alumni.** Encourage prominent alumni of journalism schools who are concerned about the climate change issue to reach out to journalism school deans and encourage them to add science journalism tracks to their curricula. Consider other access points (e.g., deans of environment schools could reach out to their peer deans at the journalism schools to build stronger bridges and cross-registration or even joint degree programs).

> **Pick the right journalists.** Some contend that the potential benefits of media training of scientists may be overstated, that talent for talking to the media is inborn, and that the world can be divided into good talkers and bad talkers. Accordingly, one solution could be a talent search to find (i.e., not to train, but to find) the best scientific talkers and to help them do more outreach.

> **Recommendation #9:** *Initiate a climate change weekly column. Find a newspaper willing to devote a weekly column to the issue of climate change and help them syndicate it to others – or work with one of the large newspaper chains to provide a larger multi-newspaper platform. Recruit a talented and ambitious writer and give him or her, in effect, a virtually unlimited budget to pursue the story.*

➢ **Secure regular outlet.** Given that at least nine out of ten Op-Ed submissions are rejected, identify ways to pre-wire an agreement to publish an Op-Ed or other popular piece so that time-starved research scientists can be encouraged to write by a higher likelihood of publication. One way to do this would be to secure a regular climate or science column. Since writing for a lay audience is already an add-on and not in the scientist's reward system, long publication odds impose a compounding barrier that might be addressed through having a reliable outlet.

> **Recommendation #10:** *Invite the media in.*

➢ **Help media find the stories in the science.** Some of the news media professionals at the Yale Conference who had not previously attended a climate change event suggested that there may be opportunities to secure more media coverage for climate change-related events and conferences by simply inviting more media people (from all media and all levels, national to local) to such meetings and then helping them find story ideas once there. While this may seem like an overly obvious "fix" to the relative lack of coverage of climate change, it is useful if it puts additional onus on organizers of even specialist meetings to consider the newsworthiness of what they are orchestrating and to engage in more proactive advance work with the media. It is quite likely that many specialist meetings are routinely considered not appropriate for the news media and so the connection is never made. In some cases, this may be warranted given the preliminary status of findings to be presented. But even here, journalists can be provided guidance on what is appropriate for coverage and what isn't, and be directed toward feature stories that humanize the researchers and their exploits across the globe, even if specific data sets or findings are not similarly ready for publication. For one thing, just having news media representatives present at a meeting may impose useful pressure on participants to speak clearly and accessibly so as not to be misunderstood or misquoted. This mutual proximity and training should help, over time, in bridging between the science and the news media.

Religion & Ethics

QUESTIONS

Religious organizations have long been at the forefront of environmental protection efforts and have recently produced open letters to legislators on climate change specifically. What impact have these efforts had, both on policy-makers and their respective religious communities?

What role, if any, should science play in such values-based mobilization?

Are greater scientific expertise and literacy needed within the religious community itself? If so, how can this need be met through practices that respect the distinct dialects spoken in the scientific and religious communities?

What role can a focal issue like climate change play in unearthing common ground between religion and science, moving the issue forward in the process?

DIAGNOSIS

> **The cross-cutting religious and moral imperative of climate change is not yet adequately recognized.** Different religious leaders and communities, with a few encouraging and relatively recent exceptions, have not yet found common ground on environmental issues such as climate change. There are possible bases for formulating common ground in the future:

> - For example, the "sanctity of life" commitment that has animated the abortion debate could be broadened to encompass risks to life from climate change. (Some counsel against this given the policy-specific meanings already associated with those words.)

> **Religious leaders do not preach on climate change.** Religious leaders rarely if ever preach on climate change, so those in their communities do not hear about it from the authority figures they trust the most. Sermons also often emphasize the past more than the future, so climate change is at a special disadvantage given this traditional focus.

➢ **Religious distrust of science.** There is a centuries-long break between science and religion, which persists to this day in the form of frequent though not uniform religious suspicion of the scientific framing of climate change and other issues.

- As a result, scientists are not always seen as credible messengers by religious groups. Scientists are often seen as portraying a meaningless, purposeless world that is anathema to religious people. Scientists are seen as having an insufficient understanding of God's love and of the power of prayer. Some scientists do bring a strong set of ethical and religious values, but religious communities do not perceive this as typical.

➢ **Specific legacy of evolution debate.** The evolution/creationism debate, in particular, has fueled religious distrust of scientists.

- Some lament this spillover from the evolution debate to the climate change debate, and know that political leaders are well aware that when they comment in favor of intelligent design or creationism, they are signaling distrust of science more broadly, including on issues like climate change.

- Others, however, see more hope embedded in the irony that naturalists/biologists and creationists are the two groups that are perhaps closest to one another on the importance of caring for nature. If they could put aside their differences over how the world began, they might find surprising depths of common ground.

- Some argue against conceding that evolutionary biology is somehow morally bankrupt and view Aldo Leopold and other Darwinists as imbued with exceptional morality.

➢ **Religious distrust of environmentalists.**

- Climate change has been framed as an environmental crisis instead of a moral or spiritual crisis. Religious constituencies are motivated especially by spiritual and social justice appeals, and the framing of the climate change issue has so far been limited in tapping those dimensions.

- Many religious groups' perception is that environmentalists are less concerned about human beings or business and job loss. Some evangelicals are more inclined to see business leaders as credible on issues like climate change because they are measuring actions against job loss potential, whereas scientists, environmentalists or even economists appear to be only theorizing about what the economic costs of mitigation will be.

- Reasons for the distrust include a view that many environmentalists are pantheists who believe the Earth is part of God or that the Earth is our "mother."

- Religious leaders are especially cautious about being hijacked for someone else's agenda, and environmentalists are among those who are perceived as having a special interest agenda, one that is culturally alien to many religious communities.

➢ **It just takes time.** Religious communities and leaders have embraced climate change over varying time frames. One religious leader at the Conference, for example, described a four-year process of coming to accept science as a truth bearer on the issue of climate change, which only then culminated in a significant statement on this issue. This is a much slower process than the accelerating march of scientific progress.

➢ **Negative emphasis of climate change message.** Some feel that the negative formulation of climate change as a threat requiring sacrifice and changes in the quality of life has undermined its ability to break through to religious communities. Evangelicals, in particular, are often repelled by calls to work with other groups associated with gloom-and-doom messages on things like population control, the need for big government, etc. Could the climate change issue be successfully reframed, one Evangelical leader asked, as an opportunity to live a more morally and spiritually fulfilling life and serve to overcome this deeper resistance?

➢ **Outdated curriculum in religious schools.** The coursework of many religious training schools and institutions has changed little in hundreds of years and has yet to make room for environmental issues.

➤ **Lack of "nature" in mainstream philosophy and ethics.** Environmental issues have not been treated prominently in mainstream curricula and texts on philosophical or ethical reasoning. This has limited the academic and literary exposure that Americans have to it in the formative years of their critical thinking skills, and later in their ongoing reading.

➤ **Inadequate elaboration of the climate-poverty link so far.** Some in the religious community perceive that social justice is de-emphasized in the policy debate on climate change. This perceived vacuum of concern about the well-being of disadvantaged populations extends, interestingly, into their interpretation of policy mechanisms such as "cap-and-trade." While policy proponents assert that cap-and-trade serves as a mechanism for promoting flows of capital from industrialized to developing countries, some in the religious community see a risk that the poor could "trade away their credits" and, in so doing, either give up their development rights or be in a situation where they need to pay up in the future to re-acquire them.

The poverty issue is global but also an issue inside the United States, as revealed by Hurricane Katrina. Katrina has highlighted how climate change may be not only an issue for elites and environmentalists but also one of critical importance to the disadvantaged.

➤ **Civil rights movement a model?** The last great engaging movement of the religious community was arguably in support of social justice during the civil rights movement. Could climate change become a similar movement?

➤ **Climate change is displaced on the agenda by other perceived spiritual emergencies.** Some religious adherents live in a state of "spiritual emergency." They are constantly aware of eternity and how the sins they commit – of commission or omission – can imperil them and risk a future in hell. Their work to establish the "sanctity of life" that they perceive to be threatened by abortion policies in America is in a prior and preemptive status at the top of their list of emergency obligations. So far, climate change is not perceived as sufficiently threatening (or even real by some) to rearrange that set of priorities. A similar agenda displacement has occurred, some suggest, among many in the Jewish community, whose primary policy focus is on Israel's survival.

- Not only is climate change displaced from the top spot on the religious agenda, in many cases it does not even make the top 10 list of their priorities. Some religious communities have ranked climate change at a similarly low position in the recent past, but then elevated it quickly upon being confronted with the science and immediately seeing its moral and religious significance. So quick turnarounds and agenda resetting can occur.

RECOMMENDED ACTIONS

The Religion & Ethics working group formulated the following preamble to introduce their recommendations.

Preamble to Recommendations

1. The current moral imperative on climate change articulated by many in the faith community recognizes that:

   a. Any action that risks the quality and viability of life on earth and future generations is fundamentally an act of destruction and morally unacceptable.

   b. Changing something as fundamental as the chemistry of the Earth's atmosphere is morally unacceptable.

   c. Any action that increases the risks to the most vulnerable is morally unacceptable.

2. America as the world's richest nation has historically and currently contributed so much to the climate change problem that it is morally obliged to take leadership responsibility to address this problem.

The religious community could help resolve this problem by adopting the following steps within their respective traditions, recognizing many have already achieved great progress.

> **Recommendation #11:** *Religious leaders and communities must recognize the scale, urgency and moral dimension of climate change, and the ethical unacceptability of any action that damages the quality and viability of life on Earth, particularly for the poor and most vulnerable.*

> ➤ **Urgency may promote commonalities.** Heightening the sense of urgency is especially important to accelerating the impulse toward finding common understandings across the religious/ scientific divide and also between religions on issues like climate change. Without urgency, the differences may continue to take precedence over commonalities.

> ➤ **Informing urgency.** Religious leaders, therefore, should be supplied not just with basic information about climate change, but especially information about the threat of non-linear change, abrupt surprises, and irreversible effects such as species extinction caused by climate change.

> ➤ **Dr. Martin Luther King, Jr.** Some have called climate change a civil rights issue for our era. One religious leader quoted King at the Conference and helped promote focus among the participants:

> "We are now faced with the fact that tomorrow is today. We are confronted with the fierce urgency of *now*. In this unfolding conundrum of life and history there is such a thing as being too late. Procrastination is still the thief of time. Life often leaves us standing bare, naked and dejected with a lost opportunity. The 'tide in the affairs of men' does not remain at the flood; it ebbs. We may cry out desperately for time to pause in her passage, but time is deaf to every plea and rushes on. Over the bleached bones and jumbled residue of numerous civilizations are written the pathetic words: 'Too late . . .'"

> **Recommendation #12:** *Religious leaders and communities should establish or expand religious coalitions on the environment and convene dialogues to develop common understandings and resources specifically on the climate change issue across different religions and moral traditions.*

➢ **Tailored to individual traditions.** In particular, leaders need to generate common understandings based on principles of stewardship, justice, protection of the vulnerable, community, reverence for life, and respect and responsibility for future generations. Such communication should be tailored by leaders to individual religious traditions.

➢ **Religious rationale for U.S. to lead.** Some religions are much more attuned to traditional development agendas, including international development, than they are to scientifically framed issues like climate change. For them, a key ethical point is that the United States must acknowledge its obligation to initiate action on climate change before developing countries can be expected to – this applied in the case of their favorable estimation of the Kyoto Protocol and may apply to future policies under consideration.

➢ **Coordinate, but reflect unique positionings.** Continue to seek to build on and even create new models like the National Religious Partnership for the Environment that attract and channel resources without tainting the unique positioning of the partnering religious groups. Such coalitions must cut out neither conservatives nor progressives.

➢ **Religion and politics.** Recognize the way that religion and politics mirror each other in the United States, and be prepared to work together both covertly and overtly on climate change.

➢ **Prayer.** A call to action should include an emphasis on prayer, and on asking for the strength to act in furtherance of God's will, but not to absolve human responsibility.

➢ **Dialogue over the Web.** Some counsel that traditional dialogues take too long to set up and execute and that modern technologies need to be harnessed to move ahead with greater urgency. Email and the Web could be used, as in *www.faithfulamerica.org.*

Recommendation #13: *Religious leaders should reach deep into their memberships to communicate the scale of the problem and the vital moral imperative of addressing it.*

➢ **Hearing from the faithful.** It is important that religious people hear about climate change from one another (including religious scientists who present themselves as such) and their religious leaders. Hearing from them will hold much more persuasive and motivational power than attempts by non-religious messengers to influence them.

> **A day to preach on climate change.** Religious leaders should use sermons, youth groups and other educational venues to educate and motivate their members on climate change. Establish a day when churches are encouraged to preach from their pulpits about climate change.

> **Be visual.** They should harness visual media as well as traditional written and oral media.

> **Supply model sermons.** Religious leaders should be provided with model sermons and other statements that they can use to provide accurate information on the issue, but also the morally and religiously appropriate context.

> **Word choices matter.** Language choices should be carefully attended to as each religious leader tailors messages to their own constituency. For example, one leader might be more comfortable talking about the "social justice" element of climate change, while another might prefer referring to the poor as "the least of these."

> **Don't just preach . . . listen.** Leaders should ask their memberships what can be done about the climate change issue.

> **Recommendation #14:** *Religious leaders and communities should communicate their concern for urgently addressing climate change to the nation's political leadership and broader public.*

> **Recommendation #15:** *Recognizing that business leaders are well positioned to promote receptivity to climate change messages among certain religious constituencies, create new opportunities for dialogue on climate change between business and religious leaders and communities.*

> **Vary the format: private and public.** The format, location and confidentiality of the dialogues should be varied to suit the issue but also the needs of the participating leaders. In some cases it is vital that quiet, one-on-one conversations happen between senior

business and religious leaders before any larger conferences are convened. However, in many cases, larger, open conferences are needed to broaden the circle of engagement, perhaps after the leader meetings pave the way.

Recommendation #16: *Establish religious outreach efforts on climate change tailored specifically to certain regions of the United States and their own religious traditions, especially the U.S. South.*

➢ **Respect regional traditions.** Each region of the country possesses its own religious interpretations, including beliefs about the proper role of the religious/political interface. Although models from past engagements by the religious community like the civil rights struggle could inform and provide a model for action on climate change, it is important to respect regional religious traditions and build on them in approaching the issue of climate change.

➢ **The South is pivotal.** Religious communities in the U.S. South might play an especially pivotal role in remedying the nation's science/action gap on climate change. The South, some note, stereotypically sees the North as a "know-it-all" region that is culturally alien. Could the South find its own rationale for solving the climate change challenge that is true to its religious and other traditions? The experience of Hurricane Katrina could be part of this.

Recommendation #17: *Continue to develop and expand the field of Religion and Ecology, and its ability to unearth the commonalities across religions on matters of ecology and to supply language, concepts and textual support to religious leaders who want to articulate environmental issues to their constituencies. (See, for example, www.environment.harvard.edu/religion.)*

Recommendation #18: *Reach out to seminaries and other religious training institutions and encourage them to incorporate climate change into their curricula for new religious leaders. Provide education on climate change to current clergy via continuing education and other means.*

> **Recommendation #19:** *Establish religion-science and religion-environmentalist partnerships on environmental issues.*

➣ **Learn from successful models.** There are issue-specific models of recent success to build on in creating partnerships on climate change. For example, scientists and religious leaders worked together to defend the Endangered Species Act in the Noah Alliance (*www.noahalliance.org*).

➣ **Inter-faith is not the only way.** This kind of engagement need not be on an inter-faith basis. Rather, given different religions' level of comfort with science, it might be more productive for each to engage individually with science in the way that suits their preferences, rather than have this engagement require a prior inter-faith understanding or consensus.

Politics

QUESTIONS

How has the flow of scientific information to and within the U.S. political establishment, and to the public to which it answers, influenced policy responses on the climate change issue?

Why has climate change become polarized along party lines?

And why, despite this polarization, has the issue been so little activated in electoral politics?

Can climate change be transformed into a bipartisan issue and, if so, what role might science play in facilitating this?

Would bipartisanship promote action commensurate with the problem, or would joint bargaining lead, in the end, to inadequate steps?

Can science meaningfully narrow the range of political opinion on an issue like climate change in an era of heightened partisanship fueled by cultural and values-based appeals?

DIAGNOSIS

> **Partisanship.** The climate change debate has been marked by sharply growing partisanship, especially since the high-profile 1997 debate over the Kyoto Protocol, when the Clinton Administration was closely associated with advocacy on the issue, and Republican resistance grew correspondingly. Polarization in the public intensified at that time and has not abated since.

  - Some feel that the party leadership on Capitol Hill has intimidated those who have sought to engage on the climate change issue by holding hearings or fashioning a bipartisan compromise. One anecdote: a Senator commonly associated with the right-wing, for example, who has grown personally convinced that climate change threatens his state's well-being and that he should take action, has reportedly been subjected to intense pressure not to act by the enforcers of party discipline. This has made it extraordinarily difficult to find a middle action on climate change. Civility and collegiality are at an all-time low, further restricting the process of dialogue that could allow new coalitions and policy compromises to emerge across the partisan divide.

- Despite these problems, the partisan divide on the issue has narrowed modestly in the U.S. Senate, with the Summer 2005 passage of a non-binding Sense of the Senate resolution favoring mandatory, market-based limits on greenhouse gases. No similar movement has been evident in the U.S. House of Representatives.

- Both Republican and Democratic governors and mayors, and others at the state and local level, have moved forward despite the federal stalemate. A key reason is reportedly that they are genuinely concerned that their state is vulnerable to climate change and are also anxious not to fall behind in the race to attract low-carbon development opportunities to their state (e.g., alternative energy companies, projects, and jobs).

➢ **Partisan or bipartisan.** There appears to be a lack of agreement among political leaders about whether to take a partisan or bipartisan approach to advancing this issue at the federal level. A key obstacle to forward movement is not just the existence of partisanship on climate change today, but disagreement among key political leaders about whether progress on the issue depends on intensifying or reducing this partisanship. Depending on their view of this question, different strategies are suggested.

- A partisan model would imply articulating and perhaps expanding the distinction between the parties on the issue, and then using this wedge to draw votes, achieve victory and pursue a mandate to assert their preferred policy over the objections of the other party.

- A bipartisan model, on the other hand, would suggest creating an "up the middle" policy approach that compromises enough on all sides to establish a basis for legislative advancements on climate change.

- Which is more feasible? More likely to attain meaningful outcomes in terms of climate change action? The proponents of the partisan approach note that this issue has become so intractably aligned with the partisan divide that any concessions or compromises are unlikely to be reciprocated and will simply further marginalize the climate change issue. Instead, they say the only way to proceed is to exercise raw political power, wake up the public about the urgent nature of the issue, create a major public demand for action comparable to that which stimulated major environmental legislation in the 1970s, pursue outright victory at the polls, and prompt a general realignment in Washington, D.C.

- Those favoring a bipartisan approach, on the other hand, prefer to detach the climate change issue from any partisan agenda so that the first and most feasible steps toward meaningful action can be passed into law at the earliest possible date – a "purple" strategy (blue state and red state). Yet it is not clear which legislators would be most amenable to a new bipartisan consensus for climate change action, beyond those already involved in the issue, and whether this aproach can therefore succeed.

➢ **Not enough advance issue mobilization before election season.** Despite the active hurricane season in Florida just prior to the 2004 elections, and evidence that global warming was linked to greater hurricane intensity, some polling in that state showed that the public did not draw a connection between their votes and global warming. There was awareness of global warming and even of the scientific link between warmer waters and intensified hurricanes, but the causal jump from voting to hurricanes was evidently more than people were prepared to make. As a result, the environmental advocacy group that commissioned this particular poll did not advertise with a global warming message, but instead focused their Florida ads on offshore oil drilling. Evidence from 2005 similarly showed that the public remained disinclined to hold their elected leaders accountable for the potential global warming link to extreme weather. Once an election season arrives, it is generally considered too late to engender public understanding to an extent that would make global warming a voting issue. If it is going to become one in future election cycles, the ground needs to be paved well in advance, particularly in light of the sequence of the documented public resistance to making the links.

➤ **Value divergence.** Liberals and conservatives are motivated by distinct and deeply rooted sets of values, which influence how they interpret and often discount information and messengers. Different characterizations of these contrasting value sets exist, including cognitive linguist George Lakoff's formulation of conservatives as favoring "strict father" values and liberals "nurturant parent" values (see George Lakoff, *Moral Politics: How Liberals and Conservatives Think*, 2nd edition, University of Chicago Press, 2002). Typically, people do not explicitly communicate their underlying value structures, which can lead to underestimation of their importance in explaining political preferences on climate change and a range of other issues.

- Liberal-leaning environmentalists are often reluctant to recognize the different value sets of conservatives and therefore fail to frame climate change in a way that connects with them. There is a set of so-called "bi-conceptuals" in the population, to use Lakoff's formulation, who share elements of both the liberal and conservative value sets and could likely be mobilized on climate change if an appropriate approach were crafted.

- Facts alone do not motivate. Environmentalists are, in the estimation of some, among the last on the planet to see this. One must drive rational points more effectively into the emotional context of people's values and where they live. A greater focus on how the consequences of climate change brush up against the lives and values of those who have so far been indifferent or opposed to action is critical to creating a larger base of concern.

- Some favoring climate change action fall into the same trap that many other political activists do, namely, reading the polls literally and following them mechanically. In doing so, they miss the chance to act authentically, based on their real concerns about this issue – which, in the end, could be politically potent in connecting to the values of American citizens.

- An example cited at the Conference: Former President Ronald Reagan won despite a gap between his issue stands and the public's issue preferences. Why? Because he was talking about issues largely as a door to what he and many others saw as a more important discussion on values – and on values, he was more closely aligned with the American public. Values are the key driver of the public's decision-making and until those favoring action on climate change do a better job of connecting to values, they will not advance the issue.

> **Lack of awareness of elected leaders' actions.** Some polling studies show that while large numbers of Americans believe climate change is a serious or very serious problem (30-34 percent, depending on the poll), they also think – often wrongly – that their leaders agree with them and are taking action, whether in support of the Kyoto Protocol or otherwise. Significant numbers of Americans appear, based on polling, to be unaware that the United States has been criticized for falling short of European commitments on climate change (*www.worldpublicopinion.org*).

> **Misguided preoccupation with the human vs. natural causation issue.** Some argue that proponents of climate change action have allowed themselves to be drawn into a debate about whether and to what extent observed climate change stems from natural versus human causes. As a result, they have not seized the issue of preparedness for and adaptation to the effects of climate change, independent of cause.

> **Spillover from media incapacity.** The media's limited and often poor coverage of climate change is sometimes blamed for political disengagement from the climate change issue. In this view, politicians respond to the agenda-setting function of the media. When the media create little space for political leadership, politicians are less likely – at least in critical mass – to step forward.

> **Failure on CAFE.** Some elected officials have asserted that opportunities to advance a bill on the Corporate Average Fuel Efficiency (CAFE) standards have been squandered recently. Both parties have failed to seize available legislative initiatives that would address greenhouse gas emissions from transportation.

> **Little constituent pressure.** Some polling of political leaders indicates that while they personally favor action to address

climate change, it has not risen to the top of their legislative agenda, in part because they are unaware of their constituents' support for action. Politicians have simply not experienced much constituent pressure to act on climate change. As a result, there are few champions of the issue, with acknowledged exceptions such as Senators John McCain and Joe Lieberman.

> **Failure to connect the problem (and the solutions) to people's lives.** Climate change has been portrayed as an issue "out there in the environment," which tends to imply that it is beyond the circle of citizens' immediate lives. Political leaders have failed to overcome this distancing effect by drawing the connections to people's personal lives. Nor have they articulated solutions that speak to Americans' personal responsibilities (e.g., energy use) or aspirations (quality of life). Some state-level politicians note that hunting is so core to people's lives in their state that those who want to advance the issue should – as the science warrants – explain the implications that climate change will have on local ecosystems and the ability to hunt in the future. If people understand that hunting is threatened, they will pay attention.

> **Environmentalists' lack of political acumen.** Leaders of social movements, including but not limited to environmentalists, tend to be so narrowly focused on their issues that they sometimes fail to understand how fundamental self-interest is to the politician's calculus. While there are exceptions, environmentalists need to be more disciplined in evaluating how politicians filter their issues by their electoral impact. Environmentalists must be able to generate a constituent base, ensure issue-based media coverage and succeed in orchestrating success in U.S. elections if they want politicians to respond. In short, they need to reduce the risks and accentuate the electoral benefits of being associated with the issue.

> **Lack of trust in science.** People typically rely on testimonials from those they trust. For many constituencies, this is not experts on climate change. Even if individuals are open to the fact that climate change is happening and that humans can cause it, as several polls have noted, they may not yet be willing to really evaluate and understand what the consequences will be, perhaps in part because they themselves don't know what to do about the problem. Psychologists have observed a tendency to discount a problem when one does not believe it is possible to do anything about it.

➢ **Safe seats.** The prevalence of safe seats in the Congress limits the opportunity for issue entrepreneurship on issues like climate change. When well over 90 percent of elected members of Congress face no plausible threat to their incumbency in the next election, they are less inclined to respond to any constituent pressure that can be mobilized on climate change or any other issue, to consider the electoral implications of their inaction or to have to evaluate a novel coalition. Translated into a diagnosis, this means that those concerned about action on climate change may not have focused enough on more fundamental forces on the political landscape that shape the issue context (e.g., gerrymandering, as well as other issues like campaign finance reform).

➢ **The sense that the environment and climate change are risky issues electorally.** In recent presidential campaigns, it appears that the nominees who had championed the environment (and climate change specifically) throughout their careers muted their support because of perceived electoral downsides. Not everyone agrees with this assessment, contending that the environment was discussed by the campaigns but not covered much in the media. But there was a stigma associated with these issues, and talking about climate change in particular rendered one susceptible to ridicule or at least to being called out of touch with the concerns of average Americans. Against this downside, there is perceived to be little compensating upside.

- Those who have championed the environment, especially Democrats, are confident that they will win the votes of anyone disposed to making the environment a driver of their vote, whereas talking a lot about the issue risks the downside of losing other voters, who might see economic risks from climate change action, especially in states that have been crucial in recent elections such as West Virginia.

➢ **Absence of boldness.** Those who favor action on climate change have not been bold enough in articulating a vision capable of motivating Americans. They have been too literal in their reading of polls and have crafted incrementalist policy solutions instead of a game-changing vision.

➢ **Perception of mitigation costs as greater than costs of impacts.** Many Americans appear to believe that solutions to climate change will be costly and painful, and will offer little by way of corresponding benefits.

- ➢ **Insufficient awareness of community interests and values at risk.** Americans are generally unaware of the potential physical impacts of climate change on their communities, so community values and motivation are not triggered.

- ➢ **Lack of awareness of solutions.** Even those Americans aware of the issue of climate change often lack a grasp of what they can do about it personally, or what actions governments or businesses can undertake.

- ➢ **Skeptics with power.** The forces opposing the dissemination of climate change information are powerful. Individual corporations and consortia of corporations have been effective at convincing segments of the public that the science is uncertain and that doing something will undermine the U.S. economy.

  - Climate change is an issue for which most citizens must rely on testimonials from others rather than on their own independent appraisal of the science. Many recognize that climate change is an arena populated by advocates, and so discount much of the evidence quoted to them. There are few verifiably independent and trusted authorities they can rely on. In this context, the drumbeat of a small group of skeptics can be very effective in inducing public inaction.

  - Skeptics have, even recently, been given influential platforms, (e.g., novelist Michael Crichton's 2005 testimony before the U.S. Senate's Environment and Public Works Committee).

- ➢ **Lag time in absorbing new science.** Many scientific findings, such as the impact of climate change on hurricane intensity, are relatively new and people have not had enough time to come to terms with their implications.

- ➢ **Too much Congressional strategy, too little public mobilization.** Those concerned about climate change have been operating with what some regard as a faulty theory of social change. There has been considerable preoccupation with crafting legislative options (e.g., for a cap-and-trade system to limit greenhouse gas emissions) at the expense of "waking up" the American people in the communities where they live and thereby creating a new constituency equation to which the politics will eventually respond.

> **Limited credibility of environmentalists.** Environmentalists lack political credibility in many sectors and regions in the United States. Nobody else has yet filled this credibility gap with respect to climate change, and many Americans are therefore left with no compelling proponents of climate action to follow.

> **Failure of leadership at the top.** Amidst all the efforts to diagnose reasons for the lack of climate change action, many Conference participants noted that it is easy to overlook the simplest one: a basic failure of leadership at the top in Washington, D.C., spanning multiple presidential administrations and across changes in Congressional control. Those who championed the issue did not always sustain this focus once elevated to higher office, while those who never championed it did not respond to the imperative of action once presented with compelling data on the risks and opportunities. There needs to be a searching examination of why this has happened in the past and how it can be changed in the future.

RECOMMENDED ACTIONS

Recommendation #20: *Design and execute a "New Vision for Energy" campaign to encourage a national market-based transition to alternative energy sources. Harness multiple messages tailored to different audiences that embed the climate change issue in a larger set of co-benefit narratives, such as: reducing U.S. dependency on Middle East oil (national security); penetrating global export markets with American innovations (U.S. stature); boosting U.S. job growth (jobs); and cutting local air pollution (health).*

> **More compelling rationales for action.** The climate change issue does not yet supply sufficient rationale for action on its own. Rather, it needs to be packaged with a larger constellation of issues that connect more easily with people's salient concerns today and their incentives to pursue profitable opportunities (see box on page 50, entitled "A Transformative National Effort on Energy").

- ➤ **Relationship to other initiatives.** Initiatives linking climate change to energy issues are already underway, such as the National Commission on Energy Policy, the Energy Future Coalition Securing America's Future Energy, and Set America Free. These other initiatives need to be diagnosed before launching another effort: Have they been successful so far, and if not, why not? Do they weight climate change heavily enough in their actions, communications and policy prescriptions? Should any incremental effort be directed toward reinforcing these other initiatives underway or launching a separate new campaign?

- ➤ **Positive vision.** Sustain a positive, can-do tone in this campaign to the extent possible.

- ➤ **Localize where possible.** Many of the messages contained in the larger campaign will lend themselves to identifying and communicating local risks and benefits.

- ➤ **Leverage-point strategy and grassroots.** A leveraged strategy focusing on political elites and opinion influencers and a grassroots campaign are equally critical. Some are skeptical that a true grassroots "public education" campaign on climate change is really possible, given resource constraints, the complexity of the issue and other factors.

- ➤ **Use the "purple" approach (i.e., combining red and blue states).** The bipartisan roots of environmental progress could be highlighted much more effectively in support of this campaign, both amidst the general public and elites. Those who know environmental history tend to be aware that leaders in both parties were critical to earlier successes, but the long shadow of recent polarization may have eclipsed this fact.

- ➤ **Highlight market-based mechanisms.** One virtue of incorporating a cap-and-trade system into any proposed policy fixes for climate change is that it builds on the successful model of the acid rain program that was created under a Republican administration (George H.W. Bush), which could help moderate the partisanship associated with such a proposed policy if highlighted properly.

- ➤ **Clean coal as part of the equation.** Some argue that the United States needs a major effort on clean coal and sequestration specifically to reduce the sense of economic risk that has led the coal industry to be generally opposed to climate change action.

> **Recommendation #21:** *Recast climate change as a moral and faith issue, not a scientific or environmental one. Catalyze a broader coalition of allies around this moral common ground.*

- ➤ **Moral framing.** While the "new energy" vision described in Recommendation #20 would broaden the coalition, another distinct kind of reframing is needed to advance action on climate change. This reframing would not seek to package climate change with another issue set, but would treat the issue singularly and in the context of values and morality.

- ➤ **Authenticity.** Particularly given the current partisanship in the United States, the moral implications of the climate change issue need to be drawn out so that authentic, conscience-based leadership can emerge. Values provide a basis for common ground and ultimately are critical to underpinning action on issues like climate change. Accordingly, this recommendation calls for reaching across typical divides and finding a basis for collaboration with communities, business, conservatives with environmental interests (such as fishing, hunting, hiking) and religious groups in an effort to reshape the politics and significantly boost public understanding and urgency on climate change.

- ➤ **New voices.** In recasting this issue, one intended outcome is that politicians may hear stronger and more informed messages of concern from *newly engaged* citizens and will thereby associate climate change less with special interests or advocacy groups.

- ➤ **Harness the idealism of youth.** Young people today are showing increasing idealism about public service and are, in the words of some at the Conference, "desperate for a cause." As such, a moral framing of climate change would be likely to harness this motivation more than a number of alternative framings.

- ➤ **Avoid alarmism.** The message of "urgency" on climate change may risk a backlash in some religious communities, according to one religious leader at the Conference. Communications about the risks of climate change can appear to be hyped and alarmist, and may thereby be discounted heavily among some religious denominations. In this view, the preferred message and approach should combine a methodical pursuit of what is feasible in today's power configuration, along with a slower buildup of outside support for more substantial action in the future.

➤ **Expand boundaries over time.** The route of fashioning a moral appeal may create the greatest potential for expanding the boundaries of what is politically possible over time.

Recommendation #22: *Increase the emphasis on adaptation and preparedness for climate change, both because it is warranted based on climate change we are already committed to, but also because it could be a back door to a more reality-based dialogue about mitigation.*

➤ **In favor:** Some believe that a preparedness agenda would trigger actual behavior on the ground because municipalities and other institutions charged with public safety would be prompted to conduct evaluations and scenario analyses, and to quantify needed resources. This activity would refocus people away from debates over the certainty of scientific projections and toward the what-if planning that is routine among professionals engaged in preparedness for a variety of threats to society. This would amount to building "national resilience," a task that could gain momentum from people's desire to do something to address the free-floating anxiety that pervades American society after 9/11 and Katrina. It would also level the playing field so that the frequently dramatized economic costs of policy action on climate change can be more fairly compared with the costs of inaction, which would include the need to scale-up adaptation activities.

➤ **Opposed:** Some are concerned that a preparedness/adaptation agenda would engender a sense of futility in the public and therefore reduce attention to prevention/mitigation. Moreover, some believe that the budget-constrained realities of the U.S. Congress (and of many states) could preclude real discussion of investing significantly in adaptation or preparedness, thereby inadvertently marginalizing the climate change issue.

Recommendation #23: *Recruit a group of party elders from both parties who are less ensconced in the gridlock of today's Washington, D.C., and would be more able to work together to promote constructive action on climate change among the incumbents in their party.*

➤ **Recapture bipartisanship.** Bipartisan cooperation on environmental protection and many other issues is a fairly recent phenomenon, having peaked in the 1970s in an initial burst of legislation. One way to move toward recapturing it could be via the strategy of identifying willing and able party elders, some of whom participated in the 1970s legislation or bipartisan legislation since then, to be part of a quiet, behind-the-scenes effort to work with the current officeholders in their respective parties and to mediate joint sessions to identify actionable compromises.

➤ **Elders can help on non-legislative action, too.** Identify concrete and feasible opportunities to create bipartisan coordination that begins outside the legislative arena, perhaps relying largely on retired elected or other government officials (e.g., have an eminent individual reach out to Bill Clinton and George H.W. Bush to consider expanding their collaboration on tsunami relief to climate change).

Recommendation #24: *Convene a group of political scientists, elected officials (and their staffers), and campaign operatives to conduct an analysis and dialogue about the connections between systemic problems in democratic governance in the United States and climate change. For example, how do campaign financing, redistricting and the lack of competitive seats and other factors influence policy performance on climate change?*

➤ **Study the fundamentals.** Some systemic issues, like redistricting to create non-competitive congressional seats, are often recognized as serious by the public but are not connected specifically to issues such as climate change. A vigorous and detailed analysis of these connections could illuminate the basis for gridlock on climate change and point the way toward new strategies. For example, a seat-by-seat analysis that evaluates both degree of competitiveness (swing district or safe seat) and elected officials' positions on climate change could reveal important patterns.

Entertainment & Advertising

QUESTIONS

Entertainment narratives, with their proven ability to engage the emotions and reach wide audiences, can influence the public's understanding of climate change science. Do entertainment vehicles help by penetrating public awareness and provoking further inquiry, or do they undermine environmental literacy by propagating inaccurate science?

Can the entertainment industry be enlisted to advance understanding of climate change science and its implications, while answering to its primary goal of entertaining consumers?

Professional persuaders in the advertising and public relations industries have mounted successful public education campaigns on many issues, and have been employed to disseminate both information and disinformation on climate change. How can their sophisticated tool kit best be deployed to engender an appropriate level of public understanding and engagement regarding climate change science?

DIAGNOSIS

➤ **Insiders talking to insiders.** People concerned about climate change seem to consist of a small community of people who just talk to each another. There has been no consistent, large-scale or effective strategy to broaden this circle or to reach a wider audience.

➤ **Limited public exposure to climate change science.** Perhaps 80 percent of the U.S. public today gets its only scientific information from the local weather report. And most weather reports don't explain how long term changes in the weather might effect their area, or how these changes may be the result of global warming. The public has little exposure to the mountain of science indicating that climate change is a serious threat to their well-being.

➤ **Yawn factor.** Scientific information is critical to telling the climate change story, but it has not been translated in an accessible or entertaining way for non-scientists. It tends to be reported in scientific journals that are read by a body of experts representing a miniscule proportion of the country.

➤ **Scientific information not reaching the most influential.** There are instances where prominent Americans have been exposed to compelling presentations of climate change science and have come away highly motivated to do something. But these epiphanies have been rare. There has been a failure to convey compelling and digestible elements of climate change science to those who are best positioned to make a difference on the issue. Some feel that we should not assume, however, that senior elected officials in Washington, who have blocked climate change action, are unreachable or immune to influence.

➤ **It's nobody's job to communicate climate science.** The lack of success in communicating about climate change is not surprising, given that it is not really anyone's job to communicate the science behind it on a systematic and ongoing basis. Crafting a communications campaign on this issue may not be rocket science, but it probably requires a centrally organized effort. Some look to a coordinating entity or even one individual to orchestrate a sustained and strategic messaging campaign. Others contend that relying on one messenger or one entity would risk narrowing the effort too much, and that different messengers and different messages are needed to reach multiple target audiences.

➤ **Limitations of environmentalists as messengers.** Many environmental groups are managed by "policy wonks," who perform important roles on issues like climate change, but may not be up to the daunting communications challenge ahead. Despite the successes environmental groups have had in the past alerting the public to specific threats, this threat may just be too massive for any one sector to handle alone. Additionally, some of the leading champions of action on climate change are discounted because of their partisanship or perceived liberalism.

➤ **No neutral entity.** Many feel that there is no trusted, neutral authority on climate change science that the media and interested constituencies can access without concerns about bias.

➤ **Inadequate resources.** With few exceptions, the resources available to communicate climate change science (money, people, and infrastructure) have simply been inadequate, particularly in comparison to the magnitude of the threat.

➤ **No repetition of key messages.** Successful issue communications require repetition of key messages, via multiple media, to effectively reach the intended recipients. Climate change communications have been small-scale and infrequent, and have not begun to approach the repetitive, immersive campaign that would be needed to generate true public attention and concern.

> **Displacement by immediate issues.** Americans routinely defer consideration of long term issues like climate change because others seem more immediate, more grave or more physically threatening (e.g., terrorism). Climate change is, in fact, physically threatening, but people have not made this connection at a visceral level.

> **Past advertising efforts on climate change not connected to action on the ground.** Why didn't a reported $12 million television advertising campaign funded by media entrepreneur Ted Turner succeed in "moving the needle" on public urgency about climate change? Some draw military analogies to explain that the campaign's aerial campaign (i.e., television advertising) wasn't adequately supported by a ground offensive (i.e., grassroots organizing). The "I Found It" evangelical campaign in the 1970s was suggested as a potential model for doing better. The media portion of that campaign directed people to get in touch with their local churches, which then executed the ultimate goals of the campaign through personal connections.

> **Wall Street Journal's position on climate change.** Some single out the adverse impact of the Wall Street Journal's editorial position against taking action on climate change, noting that it has substantially limited the business community's understanding of the issue and its motivation to act.

> **Co-benefits from addressing climate change have been underleveraged.** There has been a striking failure to tie the issue of climate change to more tangible threats from the same emissions sources, such as conventional pollutants like particulates and their impact on premature mortality. Advertising has not been sufficiently creative in establishing these links in the public mind.

> **No mainstream vehicles.** Those who have sought to communicate climate change, like documentary filmmakers, are relatively marginal figures in the American media and communications universe. They are well intentioned, but do not have a mainstream audience. Nobody is communicating about climate change to the enormous NASCAR fan base, for example.

➤ **Uncertainty about whether to emphasize fear or solutions.** Are people more motivated by fear or by hope? Some emphasize that fear is vital to creating urgency, while others say either that fear engenders counterproductive futility or that provoking fear on an issue like climate change is not possible, given the time lag before the worst consequences will be experienced.

➤ **Disinformation.** Opponents of climate change action have succeeded in their orchestrated campaign to undermine climate change science, largely because that campaign has not been discredited or overcome by a skilled, concerted and strategic effort in support of scientific integrity broadly, and climate change science in particular.

➤ **Not enough effort to reach out to diverse communities.** Communications on climate change may have been far too narrow. Although there have been some advances in connecting diverse communities to the climate change issue, the issue has still not been the basis of an inclusive dialogue. Top-down messaging campaigns are doomed to continued failure if those most at risk from climate change are not listened to upfront and their voices not incorporated.

➤ **Fragmentation of information sources on climate change.** Currently, there is no place where people can do "one-stop shopping" for information on climate change. Instead, if they are interested, they have to assemble information on their own to get the big picture. Most decision-makers and the general public don't have the time for this, so their knowledge of the issue stays incomplete.

➤ **Lack of agreement on goals.** Messaging on climate change has been stymied, in part, by lack of agreement on the intended goals. For example:

  • Is the proper goal to influence individual consumers to make responsible purchasing choices that lower their personal greenhouse gas emissions or to prompt them to exert direct political pressure on governmental and business decision-makers to make large-scale policy changes? Or both?

  • Is the target audience the general public or the elites in government and business?

- Should the "issue public" on climate change be targeted (i.e., the approximately 11 percent of Americans who say they are personally concerned about climate change, according to polling by political scientist Jon Krosnick, and who are most prone to translate their political views into behavior on the issue)? Should the Roper Report's "influentials" be targeted (i.e., the approximately 10 percent of the population who are in leadership positions in their local communities, such as serving on PTAs, city councils, etc)?

➢ **The facts alone are not enough.** Climate change communications have been skewed too much in favor of conveying facts, important as they are, and too little in tapping emotions. Insufficient attention has been devoted to developing the human-interest stories on climate change, which could offer emotional hooks for audiences.

➢ **Limited awareness of solutions by general public.** Very little has been communicated about potential solutions to climate change. People might be more motivated to accept the problem and act if they think there is something specific they can do about it.

➢ **Limited awareness of solutions by business community.** Technological solutions are on the horizon, but many in the business community have yet to recognize the profit opportunities presented by mitigation and adaptation solutions and strategies.

RECOMMENDED ACTIONS

> **Recommendation #25:** *Create a new overarching communications entity or project to design and execute a well-financed public education campaign on climate change science and its implications. This multi-faceted campaign would leverage the latest social science findings concerning attitude formation and change on climate change, and would use all available media in an effort to disseminate rigorously accurate information and to counter disinformation in real time.*

➢ **Substantial resources.** $50-100 million may be needed to fund this effort, mostly for advertising creative work and ad buys, and $2-3 million in annual costs reserved to cover the other ongoing functions. Required seed money to start the effort was estimated at $100,000 over the first year.

> **Broader base of messengers.** The campaign would recruit a range of messengers, from leaders in key sectors of society to celebrities (novel voices from the professional sports world and other popular cultural icons with credibility and prominence in target communities).

> **Target leaders.** Many feel that high-frequency messaging to leaders and other elites would have more impact than a broad campaign to the general public.

> **Vehicles.** This multi-media campaign would include a range of print and broadcast media (example: a $1 million buy of space on the Op-Ed page of the Wall Street Journal – once per week for 20 weeks). Lower-cost buys in trade journals could also be influential. Other popular culture ideas include incorporation of climate change messages into songs, concerts, movies and other visual arts.

> **Repetition and simultaneity.** Repeated exposure to the messages would be especially important, and simultaneous reception from multiple sources would favor success.

> **Visual drama.** Dramatic visual portrayals of climate change are persuasive, even in animated form (for example, one recently exhibited animation has been touted for its persuasive influence on a prominent financier: it showed reinforcing feedbacks whereby melting arctic ice lowered the reflectivity of the earth's surface to the sun, and thereby accelerated global warming).

> **Message discipline.** Even though different messages would be crafted for different target audiences, it is important to discipline the overall effort with a coordinated set of core messages so that the impact is cumulative and reinforcing.

> **Pre-testing.** Messages should be pre-tested, using not just standard qualitative focus groups, but also quantitatively rigorous methodologies. Persuasive impacts should be evaluated, along with resiliency to counter-arguments that opposing interests could launch in response.

> **Measurable outcomes.** Baseline measurements of beliefs and attitudes should be performed before the start of the effort and measured against results afterward. The best social scientists should be recruited to conduct surveys and other evaluative processes.

> **Round-the-clock monitoring.** The communications project
> would continuously scan the news media, climate change science
> findings, entertainment and advertising outlets and educational
> materials for misinformation or disinformation on climate
> change, and respond quickly to counter it.

> **Air and ground effort.** The advertising effort should be simulta-
> neously reinforced by grassroots-level activities.

> **No public face.** The communications project entity itself would
> likely have a low public profile. Its key objective would be to
> promote climate change science in a compelling and accurate way.
> The issue of climate change science would be regarded as the client
> and key resources and services of the project would be available to
> all individuals and organizations working in that field.

> **Avoiding duplication.** It will be vital to ensure that all the key
> players in all key domains are on board with this strategy and not
> institutionally threatened by it. If there are parallel initiatives
> already in process, it will be necessary to find out who is involved
> in these initiatives and to explore whether to collaborate in a
> joint, unified effort.

Recommendation #26: *Undertake systematic and rigorous projects to
test the impact of environmental communications in all media (e.g.,
advertising, documentary, feature film) on civic engagement, public
opinion and persuasive outcomes. Use these to inform new creative
work on multi-media climate change communications.*

> **Applied social science needed.** There is a shortfall in the
> application of social science methods to the understanding of the
> public's opinions on climate change. A variety of disciplines –
> including psychology, linguistics, communications and political
> science – have developed robust insights into the process of
> attitude formation, persistence, and change. While the small sub-
> field of environmental psychology has advanced in recent years,
> the amount and quality of work on climate change particularly is
> extraordinarily limited in comparison to its intellectual and
> practical significance. Accordingly, more social science research is
> needed on public attitudes and behavior regarding climate change.

> **Experimental subjects and data available.** A ready subject for
> analysis awaits in the form of many fictional and non-fictional

creative works dedicated to increasing public understanding of environmental issues, and climate change in particular. Some of these have included baseline and post-hoc audience evaluations and could offer available data for analysis. What influence have these creative works had on the public (both at large and by segment) as they have been disseminated? This influence should be evaluated both in laboratory settings and in field studies.

➤ **One page narrative.** Given the overload of scientific information about climate change, there is a need for a concise one-page, single spaced narrative about climate change that provides a compelling call to civic engagement. It should specify concisely and arrestingly what has happened and what might happen as a result of climate change, and provide solutions for what can be done. The issue should be presented in a way that draws on the cognitive psychological work on framing, and other disciplinary findings. It should be made so compelling that it would disseminate itself through email forwarding.

➤ **Yale/Sea Studios Initiative.** As part of the follow-up to the Conference, the Environmental Attitudes & Behavior Project at Yale's Center on Environmental Law & Policy is exploring the creation of a joint initiative with the Sea Studios Foundation to develop and apply social science findings about attitude formation and change on climate change to the next phase of Sea Studios' acclaimed *Strange Days on Planet Earth* television series and multi-media communications effort, which was done in collaboration with National Geographic. Planning is underway and will likely include survey work, psychology experiments and the convening of public dialogues. Several of the scholars who attended the Conference are likely to be involved.

> **Recommendation #27:** *Embed messages about climate change into a variety of existing communications channels, such as weathercasting and entertainment vehicles.*

➤ **Weathercasting.** Every day, 200 million people in America watch the weather report. For 80 percent of these people, it is their only connection with a scientific communications vehicle. Weather reporting should go a step further in connecting weather events to climate change in a scientifically credible and engaging way. Efforts should be made to reach out to the major broadcast and

Internet weather report outlets and at the American Meteorological Association to increase reportage on climate change.

- ➤ **Entertainment.** Organizations such as the Environmental Media Association are already promoting environmental messaging in the entertainment world. These efforts should be supported, funded and extended to ensure that the climate change message is embedded in existing entertainment vehicles.

Education

QUESTIONS

How successful have campaigns to remediate low levels of the public's scientific literacy been, and what more should be done to scale up such efforts in relation to climate change science specifically?

What forces have constrained the ability of the secondary and higher education systems to make climate change a greater priority, and how might they be overcome?

Should universities put greater emphasis on inter-disciplinary, problem-oriented science driven by outcomes on issues like climate change mitigation?

Have formal educational channels been underused as conduits for disseminating climate change science?

What is the role of informal education settings, such as museums and public libraries?

What blend of educational experiences are needed to provide the depth, context and experiential immersion required for an environmentally literate society capable of addressing complex challenges like climate change?

DIAGNOSIS

> **Low environmental literacy.** Despite significant efforts and improvements in environmental education, national environmental literacy persists at a low level and K-12 environmental education programs are not making the impact that they should. Weaknesses in Americans' environmental literacy are especially apparent in knowledge about climate change, an issue where key causal sequences and knowledge of basic scientific principles are essential.

> **Poor science education.** Some note that poor environmental literacy and limited knowledge of climate change are manifestations of a more profound problem with the low quality of science education in the United States. While there is occasional Op-Ed commentary about the broader problem of our students' low ranking on scientific competency tests, and sporadic

hand-wringing about what this will mean for U.S. technological competitiveness, few have noted the implications for public understanding and motivation on issues like climate change.

➤ **Boxed into natural sciences only.** To the extent that climate change is taught in schools, it is typically taught as a natural science issue, rather than through various disciplinary lenses such as ethics/morality, social studies or economics. By focusing only on the science pathway, educators have narrowed the rich variety of opportunities to connect climate change to individual students' lives. They have also made it likely that advances in climate change understanding will proceed no faster than advances in beleaguered science education generally.

➤ **Indoor kids.** For the first time, we are facing a generation of children that has not spent significant time outside, and as a result, has a more tenuous connection to the habitats, species, farms and other natural resources at risk from climate change. Children today spend an average of six hours per day in front of screens (TVs and computers). Environmental educators must contend with this altered context for their efforts.

➤ **No emotional connection.** Caring about the environment is about the heart as well as the mind. Science and environmental educators have frequently missed the emotional piece that is critical for people to connect with an issue. Connecting emotionally is especially important on climate change because the issue is so inherently abstract.

➤ **Not cumulative.** Environmental education is not sequenced so that knowledge of issues builds on lessons from years past. Because it is so sparse, it is generally taught randomly at different times in the year.

➤ **Under-trained teachers.** Many teachers, even science teachers, do not understand the climate change issue or have a science background; many are uncomfortable teaching science. Teachers are also often focused on preparing students for national proficiency tests and increasingly for the high-stakes exams mandated under the No Child Left Behind Law. Issues such as climate change, which are not considered necessary for science proficiency, are often neglected.

➢ **Scattershot education beyond K-12.** Environmental education has been too random in targeting various sectors of society. A challenge for the field of environmental education has been teaching the issue at a community or family level. Children often influence their parents on environmental issues, which may be more difficult for a complex, multi-tiered issue such as climate change if parents do not have the requisite foundational knowledge.

➢ **No coordinated adult education.** Efforts at working with adult educators and their students on climate change have been sparse and random. This includes formal degree-based education of adults in community colleges and informal continuing education courses, where climate change could be incorporated but largely has not been.

➢ **Chilling effect of partisanship on climate change education.** Some teachers have been reluctant to teach climate change in the classroom because they have become aware that the issue is charged with partisan overtones. In light of the debates over evolution in the classroom (e.g., the Kansas School Board case), these teachers may be reluctant to expose themselves to charges of teaching material that some parents object to.

➢ **Remoteness.** For most Americans, climate change remains an abstract and remote issue. Given this, it is unclear what types of educational vehicles can best present the urgency and relevancy of climate change.

➢ **Too much information.** While it seems clear that more people need to have access to information about climate change, how much information is digestible? Have those seeking to educate people about climate change loaded them up with "too much information" – the TMI problem?

➢ **Too much reliance on formal education.** It has been estimated that schools impart only 3 to 7 percent of what the average individual learns in a lifetime. Those seeking to educate the populace about climate change must identify where else they can connect with people and, in particular, find out what people take a natural interest in and will seek to learn themselves. A particularly important sector is informal adult education.

➢ **Insufficient segmentation.** Those seeking to educate the public on climate change have rarely segmented their audience in a strategic way. Some (probably small) segment of the population appears to want to invest in becoming truly educated on climate change and other environmental issues – and educational resources can usefully be invested in them. Most others can likely be placed along a continuum from marginally interested to actively resistant. Education may play a role in moderating resistance levels, but is unlikely to create active learners across this spectrum. Some environmental educators have recognized the potential value in doing more effective targeting, for example, in aiming to educate the "influentials," whom Roper has characterized as those who are active in local leadership in their community (e.g., on the PTA or town council). One Roper Green Gauge study, which measured conservation behavior, found that while only 1 in 10 average Americans fit into the highest environmental category of "true blues," a disproportionately high 4 in 10 people characterized as "influentials" fit into this category. So far, this kind of segmentation analysis has not been adequately used by environmental educators to allocate their resources and efforts.

➢ **Lack of teachable moments.** Education is often driven by "teachable moments" or hooks that connect to salient issues. Climate change offers precious few of these. This is partly a function of the relative lack of news media coverage, but it is also intrinsic to the issue's spatially and temporally distant impacts. It is possible that Katrina could constitute such a "teachable moment." Is Katrina the Sputnik of climate change education?

➢ **Not enough local input.** Climate change education has largely been a top-down issue that allows little room for local input. While there have been useful efforts to develop experiential learning opportunities around local data gathering that can be submitted to climate change scientific endeavors, these have been sporadic and limited. As a result, educators rarely see opportunities to connect classroom work to the climate change issue.

➢ **Collective action issue.** Climate change is a collective action issue, whereas some of the issues on which education has succeeded offer a tighter connection between action and outcomes (e.g., smoking, sexually transmitted diseases). Climate change requires many causal steps from individual action to outcome, which makes the educational task especially challenging.

RECOMMENDED ACTIONS

> **Recommendation #28:** *Improve K-12 students' understanding of climate change by promoting it as a standards-based content area within science curricula and incorporating it into other disciplinary curricula and teacher certification standards. Use the occasion of the state reviews of science standards for this purpose, which are being prompted by the states' need to comply with the Fall 2007 start of high-stakes science testing under the No Child Left Behind Act.*

➤ **A valuable window.** Teachers are increasingly obligated to concentrate on high-stakes exit exams and other standardized tests as a result of the accountability provisions of the No Child Left Behind (NCLB) law. In fact, after an initial focus on mathematics and reading testing, the NCLB law will require state testing on science starting in the fall of 2007, which adds new priority to the improvement and application of state science standards. State preparation for this new accountability on science education provides a valuable window of opportunity for promoting the incorporation of climate change content.

➤ **Develop content standards.** Funding should be secured as soon as possible for the specialized task of developing climate change content standards and promoting their incorporation into the state science standards.

➤ **Design climate change curricula.** Climate change scientists should be recruited to work with a selected group of leaders and instructional designers in the K-12 curriculum field to design curricula that fulfill the proposed new climate change standards.

➤ **Recruit educational leaders.** Major educational leaders and organizations should be cultivated and recruited to this effort. Organizations like the National Science Teachers Association, which promotes national standards, are currently reviewing the quality of the state science standards and helping states to prepare. The U.S. National Research Council has set up guidance for use by states in developing their assessment system. The ongoing reviews reportedly accomplished a great deal in 2005 and will continue through the start of the high-stakes testing in the 2007-2008 school year and for at least a couple of years after that.

➤ **Engage professional associations.** Leading professional associations must also be engaged specifically to understand and promote the climate change standards. One such association is the Council of Chief State School Officers (CCSSO), a nonpartisan, nonprofit organization of public officials who head departments of elementary and secondary education in the states. The Council is well suited for this task, given its mandate to develop member consensus on major educational issues and express their views to civic and professional organizations, federal agencies, Congress, and the public. Another association that could be pivotal to success in advancing climate change standards, if cultivated effectively, is the Association for Supervision and Curriculum Development (ASCD), a nonprofit, nonpartisan organization that represents 175,000 educators globally and includes superintendents, supervisors, principals, teachers, professors of education, and school board members.

➤ **Train the teachers on the climate curricula.** Teachers should then be trained specifically to teach the proposed new standards-based climate change curricula, through on-going professional development and other means. It is also proposed that climate change be promoted for inclusion in the teacher certification process.

➤ **Earth sciences and climate.** By way of background, the current state science standards address earth sciences but rarely blend in climate change. In some states, climate change receives parenthetical mention, but to ensure significant student exposure and understanding it needs to be woven in as a significant content or subject area. Making it part of the standards and the curriculum rather than an optional topic will mitigate the problem of science teachers avoiding it due to concerns that it is partisan and will provoke a parental backlash.

➤ **Strengthen science education overall.** While the priority here is on making climate change more explicit and prominent as a subject area, resources should also be invested in remedying the quality of science education overall, especially the critical thinking and analysis skills so often missing in K-12 programs. These foundational skills are important in paving the way for a sound, contextual understanding of specific issues like climate change. Evidence suggests that there is substantial room for improvement. The science standards used today in most states are inadequate for reasonable science literacy, and continuing efforts to promote application of the National Science Education Standards should be supported. The Thomas B. Fordham Foundation published a 50-state review called the State of State Science Standards 2005, showing that the reworking of state science standards in a majority of U.S. states over the past five years has not gone far enough, but that more involvement by bench scientists, better editing and emulation of the best state models could still yield appreciable benefits.

> **Go beyond science to history, social studies, etc.** While the appropriate focus of this recommendation is on incorporating climate change into science standards, the issue is inherently multi-disciplinary and should also be actively considered for incorporation into history, social studies, economics and other curricula. This broader approach is consistent with the Conference's overall emphasis on moving climate change out of its customary silos of science, environmentalism, and insider policy debate.

Recommendation #29: *Organize a grassroots educational campaign to create local narratives around climate change impacts and solutions, while mobilizing citizen engagement and action. Kick the campaign off with a National Climate Week that would recur on an annual basis.*

> **Convene educational leaders.** To launch this effort, convene a major meeting of formal and informal educators, as well as other key leaders, to identify all appropriate formats, channels and tools. Channels could include zoos, schools, museums, and church and summer camps.

> **Emphasize informal activities.** While schools would be a venue for some of the activities, this grassroots initiative would be distinct from Recommendation #28 in that it would rely not on formal adoption of curricula, but on informal activities in and around schools, especially more flexible, non-school venues where so-called "free choice" learning occurs (e.g., zoos). It could include a climate change project day in K-12 schools to harness youth interest and to get families talking.

> **Not just for kids.** This campaign would have children as a key target audience, but would also reach out to adults, family units, and especially community leaders and "influentials."

➤ **Hyper-local issues.** To overcome the acknowledged challenges of teaching about a long-term, global issue, this campaign would be optimized to feature local or what some participants called "hyper-local" issues. It would identify local topics that local citizens are already engaged on, and link climate change to it in scientifically appropriate ways.

➤ **Mechanisms for national integration.** The effort would mix these local elements with a coordinated national education strategy. All participating localities would be integrated into a nationally cohesive campaign using a variety of technology platforms, including a richly interactive webpage, group email lists, etc.

➤ **Ubiquity.** The campaign would create and distribute innovative informational or awareness products and aim to achieve the kind of ubiquity that Lance Armstrong "Live Strong" bracelets or AOL startup disks did. Wearable, symbolic products should be considered, along with distilled information devices like pocket cards with climate change facts (e.g., 10 things everyone should know about climate change) or light switch stickers about energy use and climate change, etc.

➤ **National Climate Week.** The National Climate Week kickoff could be held in September during hurricane season. The week would serve as a focal period of activity and would reduce the burden of top-down orchestration of the grassroots campaign, since all organizations could be urged to independently plan events during this week.

➤ **Hands-on engagement.** Emphasize engaging, hands-on projects that employ verified methods for effective education. Identify local competitions to devise the best and most locally appropriate ideas for activities. Some possible projects:

- Measure local watermarks and other indicators of coastline subsidence and sea-level rise;

- Chart snow frequency and snow lines;

- Measure climate-sensitive ecosystem and biodiversity changes, as in local bird counts (see Operation Ruby Throat as an example, or the annual Christmas Audubon bird counts, which are submitted to and analyzed by qualified ornithologists);

- Conduct mercury blood level tests (reflecting the co-benefits of controlling for greenhouse gases and mercury emissions from power plants and other sources);

- Initiate carbon reduction challenges for all local community college campuses;

- Map local points of climate change vulnerability and required adaptations;

- Track local indicators of seasonal timing;

- Create Boy Scout or Girl Scout merit badges that reflect applied knowledge and monitoring of climate change;

- Undertake carbon footprint measurements at different levels: family footprint, city footprint, etc.

➤ **Find sponsors.** Identify business or non-profit sponsors who could raise the profile of, and funding available to, these projects (e.g., local utilities that could incorporate some of the energy-related actions into their demand-side management or social-benefit charge programs). Another potential sponsor is the various state-wide Interfaith Power & Light organizations.

➤ **Keep winter cool.** One example of a corporate-led effort is the Aspen Skiing Company's *Keep Winter Cool* campaign for skiers, which relates climate change to both a customer/tourist and a local economic development concern.

➤ **Agile and topical.** Ideally, this effort would be agile enough to respond to teachable moments presented by natural or political events, such as Hurricane Katrina. Participating educators should be flexible enough to harness not only traditional teachers, but also TV broadcasters, weather reporters and business leaders.

Recommendation #30: *Identify and execute opportunities to incorporate climate change content into instructional technologies, devices and software products, including video games and educational simulations such as SimCity™.*

➤ **Target products.** Ensure that the products reach across a range of interest and skill levels. We now have much more ability to narrowcast to reach different youth segments than when Sesame Street became a core educational media outlet for addressing literacy broadly and we should exploit this capability.

➤ **Desktop climate simulations.** Reach out to IBM, Apple, Dell and other original equipment manufacturers to explore bundling of simplified climate change simulation models (General Circulation Models) or other climate change-related tools into the educational versions of their products. Use these platforms to expand opportunities for "citizen-science" and experiential engagement. One focus could be teaching how simulation models are calibrated in relation to real-world empirical observations and inviting users to enter local measurements into their program.

Recommendation #31: *Create a variety of academic and non-academic competitions centered on climate change, or harness existing competitions by introducing climate change as a topic.*

➤ **Debating climate change.** Make climate change policy a debate topic for established high school competitions around the country, especially in climate-sensitive areas where natural events have highlighted the policy or planning significance of the issue (e.g., Florida).

➤ **Calculating the family carbon footprint.** Launch a program whereby children and adults could participate in a competition to learn about family energy use – their greenhouse gas "footprint," calculating their energy expenses, and figuring out how to reduce energy use. This competition could be judged by a local utility and the award could be free energy.

Recommendation #32: *Following the trend toward niche channels and narrowcasting, create a TV show or entire channel dedicated to educational and engaging coverage of all dimensions of climate change, ranging from the natural sciences to policy developments in the United States and abroad.*

Business & Finance

QUESTIONS

How has climate change science influenced the behavior of the business and finance sectors?

Do business leaders have adequate direct exposure to authoritative climate change science versus intermediary translations?

Why do some businesses move down a path of voluntary action on climate change while others resist?

How often do cases of resistance stem from genuine problems of scientific translation versus other factors, such as an overriding imperative to stave off regulation?

What are the key causes and elements of business confusion about climate change science?

What role might an improved flow of climate change science – including integrated models of physical and economic costs and benefits – have in encouraging businesses not only to take voluntary action but also to cooperate in shaping a fair regulatory response commensurate with the problem?

Are business leaders convinced by the evidence of profitable business opportunities in low-carbon technologies – and what kinds of scientific and technical data might help close any gaps impeding broader commercial pursuit of this segment?

DIAGNOSIS

➢ **Little clarity about timing and impacts of climate change.** Although many business leaders have a basic grasp of climate change science, there is a pervasive lack of adequate information on the "timing" of climate change impacts – and therefore the timeline for a response. Without deadlines, it is difficult for many business leaders to focus. Some caution that business leaders' familiarity with climate change science should not be overestimated, and that many simply don't believe what they've heard. Finally, some feel that business leaders are pragmatic and focus more on the likelihood of climate change regulation, and its impact for their business, than on their personal beliefs about the science.

➤ **Perceptions of cost, but not of opportunity.** Many businesses believe that action to mitigate climate change would be economically disruptive, and at the same time they are unaware of the profit opportunities associated with low-carbon or no-carbon products and services. Given this imbalance between perceived threat and opportunity, they are not inclined to engage on the climate change issue. Moreover, while many see the benefit of delaying action, few have grasped the likelihood that delay could substantially increase costs rather than reducing them.

➤ **Lack of customer demand.** Businesses are attuned, above all, to their customers. Few businesses are hearing or experiencing demand from their retail or wholesale customers for low-carbon or no-carbon product offerings. The "demand pull" is not operating yet to drive action.

➤ **Costs to most carbon-intensive sectors.** The business community is not monolithic and indeed for some especially carbon-intensive sectors climate change regulation does pose a substantially unavoidable risk to profits (e.g., coal companies, whose foreseeable profit margin on coal reserves would likely be marked down if a carbon tax or other signal were to be imposed). Thus, while the threat/opportunity balance could usefully be rethought in many sectors, limits exist in some sectors. Some insist instead that higher-value uses for coal exist, other than combustion as fuel, and that those options are not being exploited today due to inertia and other factors.

➤ **Concerns about slippery slope to excessive regulation.** Some business leaders are concerned that acknowledging climate change or entering into a policy dialogue to address it could lead them down a slippery slope toward a cumbersome or overly stringent regulatory program. The regulatory realm is one in which their accustomed level of control is reduced, so many find it easier to "just say no."

➤ **Concern about liability.** Businesses have experienced or observed the way that past waves of liability and litigation have taken a toll on entire sectors and are reluctant to participate in making climate change another such problem. Legally oriented NGOs and entrepreneurial trial lawyers have undertaken lawsuits against businesses for damages allegedly caused by climate change, and this could expand depending on how business responsibility for the issue is framed by legislators, the courts and the general public. In this context, businesses may be especially risk-averse.

➢ **Short-term focus.** Most of the pressures to which businesses respond are short-term in nature: quarterly earnings performance, review and evaluation by securities analysts and investors, and near-term competitive threats. Few if any of these drivers in the decision-making context for businesses have signaled the need for more action on climate change. For example, utility executives have said that it is very difficult to focus on climate change unless the analysts ask them about it.

➢ **Undervaluation of risks.** Businesses have limited inclination or capacity to measure the long-term business impacts of climate change and therefore few make a decision to disclose it as a material exposure or liability, unless shareholder action prompts them to do so.

➢ **Active opposition by threatened minority.** Many business leaders have been lumped in with the most threatened minority of the business community, whether through trade associations or an assumption by outsiders that they are part of a monolithic block. Some say that this amounts to a variation of the "tyranny of the minority" problem. Few business leaders have taken steps to disassociate themselves from disinformation campaigns on climate change science mounted by others, even when they disagree with those campaigns.

➢ **Faith in technology (and other variants of overconfidence).** Business leaders are often inclined – due to favorable experience with technology advances – to have faith in technology's ability to help society mitigate or adapt to climate change, which can undermine the impetus to take action of other sorts. More broadly, business leaders are among those with greatest confidence in their problem-solving ingenuity, which needs to be turned from a basis for inaction and delay to seeing the problem as an outlet for their skills.

➢ **Definition of climate change as an environmental problem, and associated business/environmentalist antagonism.** While some are working to change this, the issue of climate change has long been associated with environmentalism, which has caused it to be subsumed within the antagonistic dynamics between business and environmentalists.

➤ **Perverse incentives in utility sector.** Many utilities still face perverse incentives, whereby they reduce their profits if they establish demand-side efficiency programs that reduce the amount of energy they sell. Some state utility commissions have addressed this by fashioning policy reforms that decouple utility profits from megawatt hours sold.

➤ **Business leaders concerned about climate change are not yet ready to actively reach out to their peers.** It would be helpful if those business executives who have begun to address climate change could speak to those who are neutral or resistant, including exposing them to the science, impacts and economics. Despite the need for this peer-to-peer dialogue, some of those most engaged on climate change have, so far, said they are not yet ready to reach out and enlarge the circle.

➤ **Climate change is not conceptualized and communicated enough as, fundamentally, an issue of energy.** Some argue strongly that climate change has not adequately been equated with energy in the minds of business leaders. As a result, the issue has been fraught with more baggage and complexity than necessary. Some even note that a phrase like "It's the energy, stupid," would help crystallize this. Once energy is recognized as the linchpin, the debate can be reformed as profit-making opportunities (for many but not all sectors) and interconnections with other valued goals like energy independence, jobs, national security, etc. can be made.

➤ **Limited business analytics for addressing environmental risks.** Businesses routinely lack a basis for integrating environmental costs and risks – especially novel ones like climate change – into their standard accounting and other decision-support analytics. In cases where no price signal is yet associated with an environmental cost – as in the lack of a price on carbon in the United States – businesses have little systematic capacity for anticipating and acting on these costs. Energy price volatility is prompting a reexamination of exposures and trends in the U.S., a process that would benefit from including related factors like carbon price and liability anticipation.

➤ **Not enough time.** Sometimes the simplest explanations are the most powerful. The exigencies of corporate leadership leave little time to think about issues like climate change. Immediate topics like the next marketing campaign or the new product roll-out tend to be all-consuming.

➢ **Inertia, especially stranded assets.** Businesses experience considerable inertia because of normal organizational issues and the fear of regulations that could strand long-lived capital. Once you have invested in a huge coal-fired power plant, for example, it's more expensive to shut it down than to keep operating it.

➢ **Lack of regulation.** Some believe that there should be regulation to create a common playing field. Without regulation, climate change action is impeded by a fundamental collective action problem: Why move first if your competitors might not? You'll not only risk being at a competitive disadvantage, and you won't really mitigate the climate change problem itself.

➢ **First-mover risks.** Businesses are understandably reluctant to be first-movers and find themselves at a competitive disadvantage vis-à-vis others in their sector who are hanging back. For those that nonetheless consider getting out ahead of their peers, there are risks of exposing information about operations as part of a baseline emissions inventory or other early steps on the path to action, which then elicit unwelcome scrutiny and complaints of timidity from NGOs.

➢ **Risks of political retaliation.** The politicization of the climate change issue has reverberated through the business community. Some business leaders have been privately told not to take a forthcoming stance on the issue by politicians who are important to their ability to get things done, such as the permitting of new facilities. This is a sort of "upside down" democracy, where politicians are lobbying their constituents.

➢ **Lack of national U.S. leadership.** Given the relative absence of national political leadership on climate change, business leaders have little reason to believe that a regulatory program is likely to be applied in the near-term. Some who have invested in environmental finance opportunities abroad created by the Kyoto Protocol say they frequently see how much the rest of the world is looking to the United States to assume a market-shaping leadership role.

➢ **Letting business off the hook.** While the lack of national political leadership is frequently described as a key obstacle to meaningful action on climate change, some business leaders note that a predominant focus on the political vacuum may "let business off the hook." Some even say that business needs to get together and assume the leadership role and until it does, the government will not move forward. So the path forward appears stymied, in part, by the "who goes first?" problem.

➤ **Environment seen more as a PR issue than a real one.** Some business leaders do not see climate change or other environmental issues as arenas requiring significant engagement or performance, because the issues have become overly associated with PR or other corporate reputation-enhancing activities. To the extent that climate change is regarded as part of triple bottom line reporting or other reputation-oriented activities, it may not get the serious, executive consideration that the science and economic risks indicate is warranted.

➤ **Perception that climate change impacts could actually help business.** Some business leaders in climate-sensitive sectors anticipate that climate change could actually help their businesses and so are especially disinclined to do anything to mitigate the risk. For example, some in the ski industry have reportedly said privately that slightly higher temperatures would mean more time in the optimal temperature range for snowfall, which they would welcome.

➤ **Inclination to wait for definitive impacts.** Some in the business community say they're "deeply concerned" about the climate change issue and "when it starts happening, we'll address it." This approach works for many problems, but not for problems like climate change with a long lag time between cause and effect.

➤ **Trade association dynamics often favor inaction.** Trade associations are often inclined to choose a position on issues like climate change that will engender the least resistance from among their membership. In this least-common-denominator calculus, noisy opponents are often sufficiently influential to prevent taking action.

RECOMMENDED ACTIONS

> **Recommendation #33:** *The Business & Finance working group at the Conference composed the following eight-principle framework, and proposed that it be disseminated broadly to trade associations and individual business leaders (especially at the CEO and board level) as a set of clear and feasible actions that businesses can and should take on climate change.*

EIGHT PRINCIPLES FOR CORPORATE ENGAGEMENT ON CLIMATE CHANGE

1. **Analyze and disclose financial risks and opportunities related to climate change.** Undertake a comprehensive review of carbon emissions associated with products, facilities and transportation, and analyze related financial risks and opportunities, including the pro forma impact on P&Ls and balance sheets. Financial analysis will factor in the potential costs of carbon under different scenarios.

2. **Develop company-wide plan to address climate change risks and opportunities.** Develop a plan and transparent process for addressing and setting goals for reducing CO_2 emissions. Goals must be meaningful, including taking advantage of business opportunities. The plan must deal with overall carbon emissions from business activities over the short and long term, including specific plans for products, facilities, transportation, and suppliers.

3. **Educate CEOs and board members.** Provide scientific and financial education of CEOs and relevant corporate board members.

4. **Educate customers.** Educate customers on the carbon composition of products through websites, labels, bill stuffers, as it relates to the relevant business.

5. **Require major suppliers to adopt principles for corporate engagement on climate change**.

6. **Engage in policy dialogue at the state, regional and national levels.** Support efforts to build a market-based, long-term plan to address rising greenhouse gas emissions. Business leaders should establish an internal and external dialogue to discuss the following propositions:

   a. The scientific evidence of climate change is sufficient to justify that action be taken now, in a planned way, in order to avoid later, deeper cuts that could seriously damage the economy.

   b. Support a long-term goal for global greenhouse gas emissions from all segments of the U.S. economy at or below today's levels by 2050.

   c. Use a broad-based approach to achieve this goal, including market-based mechanisms, innovative technology, education, and informed and supportive policy development.

   d. Support international action, with the United States leading the debate through diplomacy abroad and by example at home.

   e. Continue scientific research on climate change, and amend policy and practices as scientific consensus warrants.

   f. Assure honest and fair deliberations in policy debate, and take steps to limit manipulation of scientific information or other dishonest discourse.

7. **The investment community should require clear financial analysis related to climate change from publicly traded companies and develop its own competency for analysis of corporate risks associated with climate change.**

8. **Insurance companies should assess the financial impact of climate-related events.** Given the far-reaching impact of climate-related claims, insurers and re-insurers should provide historic and forward-looking risk assessment and a plan for addressing increasing claims and adjust pricing of policy based on revised and updated data.

Commentary and Actions in Support of Recommendation #33

➢ **The vision.** See the vision statement on page 50, entitled "A Transformative National Effort on Energy." Many at the Conference agreed that this statement could serve as a highly motivating preamble to the eight principles.

➢ **A place to begin.** The level of engagement of corporate leaders on climate change needs to be substantially intensified – now. Many business leaders have refrained from taking steps on the issue due, in part, to its enormity ("too big and complex"). Put simply, they are vaguely concerned about climate change, but do not know where to begin. Therefore, the group aspired to supply a focal set of principles to overcome this particular start-up obstacle and fashion a path forward.

➢ **Validating the need.** One influential corporate leader said: "If I had something that I could take to everyone in my trade association to get them thinking about climate change, that would be great." This moment was a key inspiration for composing the eight principles.

➢ **Implementation guide.** The group debated whether a new agency would be helpful in disseminating the principles, but concluded that a better approach would be to commission a neutral entity to produce an "implementation guide" that would assist a company in implementing some or all of the eight principles.

➢ **Coordinating approach for NGOs.** Major non-governmental organizations (for example, NGOs like Environmental Defense and NRDC, both with considerable budgets dedicated to climate change) could consider joining forces on the eight-principle framework, or a comparable statement, in order to send a unified message to business and increase the likelihood of constructive engagement.

➢ **The Business Roundtable as a venue.** There may be particular business organizations or trade associations that could be key agents for disseminating or creating a set of dialogues on the eight action principles. The Business Roundtable, for example, has a modest effort underway on climate change, and it is possible that expanding on this could be worthwhile. A subsidiary recommendation, then, is to take the eight principles to the Business Roundtable and explore their interest in partnering to promote their implementation.

➤ **Private dialogues.** Whether or not trade associations become a platform for dialogue on the eight principles, a parallel effort should be undertaken to orchestrate private, peer-to-peer dialogues about them between business executives. This would entail asking those leaders who agree to undertake implementation of the principles to also reach out to the handful of fellow executives to whom they are closest, encouraging them to follow a similar process of engagement.

➤ **Segmentation into leaders and laggards?** Some favor segmentation of the business community into leaders and laggards, so that those who are prepared to move rapidly toward implementation of the principles can do so without being held back by those who are resistant. A "leader strategy" could create virtuous cycles whereby role models of engagement and constructive action attract others to follow, whereas a "consensus strategy" could hamper progress as the community conforms to the least-common-denominator approach.

➤ **Dissociate from disinformation.** Some want to make Principle 6(f) even more pointed, by encouraging businesses to explicitly dissociate themselves from scientific disinformation campaigns and also coordinated business efforts to stall or weaken formative state and regional policy efforts such as the Regional Greenhouse Gas Initiative in the U.S. Northeast.

➤ **Internal or external focus?** Some favor use of the principles primarily to guide internal dialogue and action at their respective companies, while others favor a more externally coordinated effort to fashion a critical mass of supportive businesses.

➤ **Downside of disclosure emphasis.** There is vigorous debate about whether Principle #1's emphasis on "disclosure" is a good idea. Many assert that it is consistent with Sarbanes-Oxley and the move toward greater corporate transparency regarding material risks. Others say that "disclosure" would "turn off" businesses immediately and sour their readiness to engage on climate change, especially those whose trade associations have sought to diminish a variety of disclosure requirements. Compliance costs with Sarbanes-Oxley have been high and unwelcome, so anything that threatens to compound that burden and associate the climate change issue with it should be carefully weighed. However, disclosure was ultimately included in the set of principles, in part because it will help businesses themselves to better understand their long-term risks, and other stakeholders such as investors and analysts are anxious to obtain data that can inform their activities.

➤ **No carbon jargon.** The importance of avoiding "carbon jargon" was emphasized. Policy insiders have shaped an intricate and technical dialogue about climate change, one that is not always accessible to business leaders and others for whom climate change is not a full-time preoccupation. Therefore the group sought to strip jargon out of the eight principles and also said that subsequent dialogues based on those principles should be similarly plain-spoken.

➤ **Package or piecemeal?** Implementation of the framework could proceed with an assumption that it is a package deal, or instead be meted out piecemeal. Some are particularly interested in advancing one or two of the principles in greater depth, while others say that the packaging of an integrated framework for business action is the critical value in this endeavor.

➤ **Partnership, not antagonism.** The group widely believed that there was a need to move away from antagonistic and combative approaches to environmental issues and toward a partnership or consensus-based model. Climate change, they said, is an appropriate issue on which to exercise new forms of partnerships with willing organizations, and the eight-principle framework is intended to be a vehicle for advancing this model.

> **Recommendation #34:** Create and fund an R&D organization to undertake and disseminate credible and independent studies of the economic impacts of climate change on business sectors and specific businesses at a level of detail sufficient to affect decision-making. The organization would complement this data by also offering credible information on available solutions, especially energy efficiency investments with rapid paybacks and high rates of return.

➤ **A credible information base.** Climate change has been an issue fraught with relatively superficial messaging battles, and it is important to establish an information base that will allow all players, especially business leaders, to go deeper to a level of practical action and problem-solving. The proposed R&D organization, if created, would be consistent with this emphasis and would provide critical support to businesses seeking to implement the eight principles.

➤ **Methodologies.** A variety of methodologies would be used, including scenario analyses of different energy prices and regulatory developments, pro forma P&Ls reflecting different carbon prices, and others that would assist businesses and investors in making more informed decisions. In particular, these efforts should produce greater clarity on what carbon price levels globally would trigger different strategic decisions about capital investments, so that businesses would have greater comfort that they understood the regulatory implications of different outcomes (e.g., at a carbon price of $20/ton, would a given utility find coal gasification plants a good investment?).

➤ **Build on high-quality work of others.** On the solutions side, this organization would promote and build on findings from creative organizations that incubate or spotlight low-carbon alternatives, such as the Rocky Mountain Institute and The Climate Group.

➤ **War chest to defray first costs.** Some portion of the organization's funding could be dedicated to a "war chest" for funding grants to help specific businesses defray first costs associated with energy efficiency and other emissions-reductions investments identified or promoted by the R&D organization. This part of the organization's finances could become self-funding if the initial investment was repaid during the payback period and reinvested.

Recommendation #35: Launch a certification program and logo signifying climate-friendly products and services, or rationalize such efforts already in existence in order to concentrate consumer awareness and purchasing power on behalf of climate change mitigation objectives.

➤ **Tie climate change to energy use.** The intent of the new certification and logo would be to more effectively tie climate change to energy use in the public mind. Although certifications with retail logos do exist for energy-saving appliances, renewable "green" power and carbon offsets, there may be room for improvement in rationalizing these efforts, verifying their emissions reduction value and enhancing their marketing to maximize consumer penetration.

Environmentalists & Civil Society

QUESTIONS

Has the organized environmental community mismanaged the climate change issue, as some have asserted?

Should environmentalists devote more attention to building coalitions with other constituencies, including for such purposes as communicating credibly on scientific matters?

Why have other so-called epistemic communities (e.g., foreign policy) largely left the climate change issue to the environmentalists?

How can social science findings and historical experiences from other scientifically-grounded issue campaigns inform efforts to achieve citizen-driven change on the climate change issue? What accounts for the gap between state action and federal inaction?

DIAGNOSIS

The diagnoses in this category address both challenges intrinsic to the climate change issue and ways in which environmental organizations and civil society may not have managed the issue as effectively as possible to date.

> **The science of global climate change is complex.** Previous environmental victories were based on issues involving relatively simple and attributable chemistry or impacts. The hole in the ozone was caused by CFCs. The Cuyahoga River caught fire because of flammable contaminants in the water. Climate change science, by contrast, is based on thermodynamics and is profoundly more complex and encompassing. The uncertainties and complexities of projection modeling make climate change a far more challenging issue to comprehend and communicate. This is compounded by the cumulative nature of the problem, the failure to reach consensus on what can be considered safe levels of greenhouse gases and what should be considered unsafe, as well as the difficulty of attributing isolated weather events to the changing climate. These uncertainties make it difficult to generate a higher level of clarity and urgency among the general population.

➤ **Level of urgency is unknown.** Climate change is widely perceived to be a slow, geological-scale problem. While evidence of non-linearities indicates that changes and impacts may occur much faster than is widely perceived, the issue remains afflicted by uncertain timeframes and corresponding confusion about the urgency of action. According to some, environmental groups in the United States were not immune to this uncertainty and were similarly late to wake up to the urgency of climate change, only starting to focus on it in the late 1980s.

➤ **Issue is displaced by politics.** The change in Presidential administrations in 2001 and the political capital created by 9/11 reconfigured the power structure in Washington, D.C. Legislative proposals by the Bush administration on the environment have taken environmental organizations' focus away from championing their own new legislation on climate change to defending the progress they have made in earlier periods.

➤ **Oppositional history has hampered needed alliances.** The general legacy of distrust between business and environmentalists – and the specific history of the scientific disinformation campaign on climate change sponsored by a segment of industry – has hampered the creation of new solution-oriented alliances across the divide.

➤ **New paradigm needed.** Environmental organizations failed to recognize the paradigmatic departure needed on climate change. Environmentalism has evolved historically from the conservationist first wave, through the dust bowl push for soil conservation, through to the Rachel Carson-inspired Earth Day and modern environmentalism. In this context, one could see global warming as the animating issue behind a potential new environmentalism: one in which entire ecosystems are at risk, new levels of integration with energy and economic planning must be undertaken, and the relative neglect of American stewardship is thrown into greater relief. Redefining the issue in this way requires stepping back and forging a new vision. So far, this has not occurred in the organized environmental community.

➤ **Inadequate resource commitment.** Environmental organizations are responsible for a tangible shortage of budgetary and resource commitments to climate change to date.

➤ **Too top-down.** Environmentalists have been prone to top-down communications that promote their own ideas, and are not especially effective at listening to individuals and valuing their experiences. Some think that the public would move faster on climate change if their experiences drove their opinions on the issue. This is especially complicated on an issue like climate change, where local experience is not always indicative of the larger global patterns or trends. Yet community-based citizen science (e.g., measuring ecosystem impacts, bird populations) could usefully become more central to environmental groups' mobilization strategies.

➤ **Limited self-awareness of the limits of their credibility.** Environmental groups have not fully understood how limited their credibility is among certain target audiences. As a result, they have not done enough to broaden their membership or to work in quiet collaboration with others.

➤ **Lack of political savvy.** With some exceptions, environmental groups have not been especially effective at political mobilization. Some note the high level of fragmentation among environmental groups and compare them unfavorably to the National Rifle Association, which builds and harnesses its influence through disciplined political mobilization, allocation of resources to defeat candidates who oppose their favored policies, and message consistency at all levels.

➤ **International focus to the exclusion of domestic issues.** While the environmental movement is large, it tends to be engaged at any moment on a limited set of issues. Prior to the Kyoto Protocol, the movement concentrated largely on the international process regarding climate change and did not commit sufficient energy to building support for a program of domestic emissions limits. This mobilization gap has limited the level of public engagement on the issue.

➤ **Individualist model.** Environmentalism has often been based, like many other movements, on the individual, rights-based model that dominates legal analysis and remedies. This model is not especially well suited to organizing on an issue like climate change, where communities and entire nations are a more appropriate unit. Environmentalists have not done enough to coordinate with religious organizations, for example, which are closely intertwined with the community level of organization.

➢ **Professionalization of environmentalism has sapped vigor.** The environmental movement itself has been increasingly professionalized. As a consequence, inertia has set in and some would contend that a degree of passion has been lost. Some environmentalists have grown less willing to think outside the box.

➢ **Climate change has not been linked to distributional and health effects.** Many successes of environmental mobilization and policy advancement have been driven by highlighting the adverse health effects of an issue, especially on vulnerable segments of the population such as children or the poor (for example, the Food Quality Protection Act passed largely due to highlighting of exposures in children). Others include the impact of cigarettes, diesel emissions and lead on children. Another example is the impact of the atomic weapons' testing program on island populations. So far, the distributional and health impacts of climate change have not been portrayed effectively in the United States, leaving a motivational gap. Opportunities exist to tie climate change and heat stress to impacts on the poor, including interactions with local air pollution and asthma.

➢ **Narrow framing of the issue.** While framed as an environmental issue, the implications and consequences of climate change reach beyond environmental transformations. The climate change story has many human dimensions, including social, political and security. Environmentalists are not necessarily the most effective message-bearers of these interconnected issues.

➢ **Membership base not broad enough.** Environmental groups have not reached out to a sufficiently broad base on the climate change issue. As a result, the impact of the movement on the national leadership has been limited. The environmental movement's membership and audience may not be what is required to secure action on the climate change issue. A radically different base may be required.

➢ **Technocratic emphasis fails to harness moral energy.** Many environmental groups are creatures of their early successes, in that their primary modes of action are driven by forms of policy and legal engagement that reward technocratic expertise, but do not harness the moral energy of the public or their leaders. Climate change is especially well suited for moral engagement, but there is a question whether environmental groups will be able to leverage this dimension of the issue.

➤ **Lacking vision, theory and models of "social change."** Success in previous social movements has come from tapping into the nation's deepest hopes, convictions or moral obligations. Efforts to mobilize Americans on climate change have done none of this, at least not effectively. Environmental organizers have not looked enough to successful examples like the civil rights movement.

➤ **Too "inside the beltway" and not coordinated enough on state/local actions.** Environmental groups have focused at the federal level on specific policy and legislative issues, but have not been as effective at deploying their top talent to support state and local actions on climate change.

➤ **Limited sectoral focus.** Many environmental groups that focus on climate change have been focused on one or two sectors (e.g., the oil or utility sectors) and have focused less on other important sectors, (e.g., the automotive and service industries). This has galvanized a degree of opposition from those concentrated industries and has understated the multi-sectoral aspect of any national solution.

➤ **Lack of coordination across the sectors.** A fundamental disconnect exists between the nature of the issue and the way the movement is organized. Environmental organizations have not done a good job of working in partnership with each other. Seen in the big picture, the environmental movement is a loose alliance of very small organizations. By contrast, opponents who believe their interests are directly threatened by action on climate change include extremely large, well-funded organizations with strong leaders who act quickly and effectively in responding to both internal and external challenges.

➤ **Lack of strategic communications.** The communications efforts of most environmental communities on climate change have not been strategic and have not adequately leveraged empirical research techniques to pre-test messages with target audiences. Environmental groups have, with few exceptions, not done enough to combine resources to craft a common, or at least mutually reinforcing, message on climate change.

RECOMMENDED ACTIONS

> **Recommendation #36:** *Create a broad-based Climate Action Leadership Council of 10-12 recognizable and senior eminent leaders from all key national sectors and constituencies to serve as an integrating mechanism for developing and delivering a cohesive message to society about the seriousness of climate change and the imperative of taking action. The Council would include leaders from business, labor, academia, government, the NGO sector, the professions (medicine, law, and public health) and community leaders. They would be chosen on the basis of their credibility within their respective communities, but also across society at large.*

> ➤ **Persuasive rather than formal power.** The Climate Action Leadership Council would help to create a broader base of national concern and support regarding climate change action, and would judiciously consider a variety of proposed near-term and long-term strategic actions that their various communities could seek to undertake on the issue. The working group did not seek to create a detailed blueprint for governance that would clarify what, if any, organizational power the Council would have with regard to their own organizations or others that might be seen to fall under the Council's umbrella, specifically on climate change. The general emphasis appeared to be on the Council's persuasive influence, rather than its formal power.

> ➤ **The strong centralized model.** At least one member of the working group insisted that the proposed Leadership Council model would likely perpetuate the diffusion of responsibility and ineffectual leadership that has afflicted the climate change issue. In this view, a true centralization of power and funding is needed to prompt a real and dramatic upgrading in the handling of the climate change issue, most likely in the form of a new organization. This organization would be endowed with sufficient resources and probably a non-environmentalist leadership capable of penetrating and mobilizing new segments of society.

> ➤ **The looser council model.** While this proposal for a new organization was carefully considered, the working group appeared to lean toward the looser Leadership Council model. It

should be noted that what the two options shared is their emphasis on greater integration and coordination on climate change across many constituencies, rather than the arguably diffuse, non-cumulating efforts that have slowed progress to date. Where the two parted company was on the degree of centralization and resource control required for success.

➢ **Flexibility and coalitional agility.** The Leadership Council model was favored, in part, by those who thought it would maximize strategic flexibility and agility. It could, for example, reach out to other leaders to devise political strategies to achieve agreed outcomes but without insisting on inclusion of an overt climate message. The group's very diversity could discipline it to focus on outcomes, rather than issue entrepreneurship and brand-building on behalf of their own organizations. For example, the Council might reach out to coordinate with public health leaders on messages or actions related to the risks of certain power generation sources, or join with labor leaders on a strategy to reinvigorate the auto industry around more competitive cars for a low-carbon future.

➢ **Behind-the-scenes activities.** Opinions on how visible the Council should be vary. Some believe that its public profile would be critical to its persuasive impact, while others think it could usefully perform a number of backstage coordination roles to add coherence to what has been a fragmented effort on climate change so far, without threatening the turf of any participating organizations. These roles would include establishment of shared objectives (e.g., contents of national legislation or an international agreement they would favor), message coordination, fundraising and recruitment of marketing talent.

➢ **Kickoff event.** The kickoff event for the creation of the Climate Leadership Council could be to convene one or more leadership conferences among a wider group of prominent leaders to ask and address the fundamental questions on climate change: Whose job is it to lead? What is the solution list? What can people do? This would air out key issues, and also provide an audition of sorts — the strongest performers at these meetings would be candidates to be on the Council itself.

➢ **Target audiences.** Climate change is most likely to strike a chord with those whose interests are affected by changes already underway that may be attributable to climate change. Messages should be especially crafted to resonate with these groups, and should cover multiple areas of concern, such as health, security, the family, etc.

> **Link to the Earth Charter.** The Council may want to consider creating a values statement that is linked explicitly to the 1992 Earth Charter, so that it would be grounded in common global ethics.

> **Common goal.** The Council would specify a common goal that it can rally around, e.g., to achieve near zero net emissions in the United States by a specified date.

> **Speaker's bureau.** The Council would create and staff a speakers' bureau to communicate effectively on climate change, with an emphasis on recruiting locally compelling scientists and other experts.

   • *Benchmarking.* Start by benchmarking against the successes and learnings from previous or ongoing efforts, such as the Greenhouse Network, a training and speakers' clearinghouse on climate change. Evaluate, for example, the record and experiences of the U.S. National Assessment on Climate Change, which used credible local institutions as staging grounds for their dialogues.

   • *Messaging handbook.* A glossary and message bible should be developed to assist with communicating climate change science and related messages to different constituencies.

   • *Positive messages.* The group generally felt that the void of positive messages needed to be filled to strengthen communications on climate change. Projections of doom-and-gloom have, on this account, created audience fatigue, whereas more positive framing with inspiring stories of how the problem is being addressed have been scarcer. Put simply, the message needs to be communicated less as the "sky is falling" and more as the "little engine that could."

> **Recommendation #37:** *In order to scale up and bring in the required resources, expand the number of donors who understand the urgency of climate change and work with them to identify action-oriented grants consistent with their funding mission and style.*

> **Recommendation #38:** *Create an environmental corps of college students to lead research and action on climate change. This would range from promoting greenhouse gas reduction pledges by their respective colleges and universities to undertaking action beyond their institutions.*

- Energy Action, a network of college organizers, has been formed and is making impressive progress, so the recommendation should include a plan to evaluate this and other college-level initiatives, with an expectation that they may be augmented and further coordinated with one another in lieu of creating a new corps.

> **Recommendation #39:** *Create one or more competitions among the 200+ U.S. mayors who pledged to voluntarily fulfill the Kyoto Protocol target, whereby their cities would seek to best one another on some specific and measurable climate change-related metric, such as the most compact fluorescent light bulbs installed within a year.*

Summary List of Recommendations

Yale School of Forestry & Environmental Studies Conference on Climate Change
October 6-8, 2005

SCIENCE

Recommendation #1: Create a new "bridging institution" to actively seek out key business, religious, political, and civic leaders and the media and deliver to them independent, reliable and credible scientific information about climate change (including natural and economic sciences). *(p. 110)*

Recommendation #2: Reorient research priorities on climate change to be more responsive to society's information and decision-making needs, including greater emphasis on impacts, local consequences, timing, non-linear risks, adaptation, and solutions. *(p. 115)*

Recommendation #3: Strengthen citizen-science initiatives on climate change so as to build greater public engagement with the conduct of climate change science. *(p. 116)*

Recommendation #4: Identify and execute feasible, high-level actions that could modify the financial and reward structures within academia most responsible for inhibiting: a) interdisciplinary and problem-oriented research on large-scale, urgent issues like climate change; and b) faculty and PhD student engagement in public communication, policy-making and other public service arenas. Recruit key influencers to meet with university presidents, university funders, and other influencers in furtherance of this objective. *(p. 118)*

Recommendation #5: Identify mechanisms to preserve and advance the integrity of the publicly-funded scientific research enterprise, especially on climate change. Shine a public spotlight on the process by which the federal science agenda is developed and funding choices are made. *(p. 119)*

Recommendation #6: Convene one or more dialogues free of economic and political compromises to undertake a fundamental redefinition of the climate change challenge in light of its urgency. *(p. 119)*

NEWS MEDIA

Recommendation #7: Educate the gatekeepers (i.e., editors). In order to improve the communication of climate science in the news media, foster a series of visits and conferences whereby respected journalists and editors informed on climate change can speak to their peer editors. The objective is to have those who can credibly talk about story ideas and craft reach out to their peers about how to cover the climate change issue with appropriate urgency, context, and journalistic integrity. *(p. 126)*

Recommendation #8: Enhance the scientific competence of journalists. *(p. 127)*

Recommendation #9: Initiate a climate change weekly column. Find a newspaper willing to devote a weekly column to the issue of climate change and help them syndicate it to others – or work with one of the large newspaper chains to provide a larger multi-newspaper platform. Recruit a talented and ambitious writer and give him or her, in effect, a virtually unlimited budget to pursue the story. *(p. 129)*

Recommendation #10: Invite the media in. *(p. 129)*

RELIGION & ETHICS

Recommendation #11: Religious leaders and communities must recognize the scale, urgency and moral dimension of climate change, and the ethical unacceptability of any action that damages the quality and viability of life on Earth, particularly for the poor and most vulnerable. *(p. 136)*

Recommendation #12: Religious leaders and communities should establish or expand religious coalitions on the environment and convene dialogues to develop common understandings and resources specifically on the climate change issue across different religions and moral traditions. *(p. 136)*

Recommendation #13: Religious leaders should reach deep into their memberships to communicate the scale of the problem and the vital moral imperative of addressing it. *(p. 137)*

Recommendation #14: Religious leaders and communities should communicate their concern for urgently addressing climate change to the nation's political leadership and broader public. *(p. 138)*

Recommendation #15: Recognizing that business leaders are well positioned to promote receptivity to climate change messages among certain religious constituencies, create new opportunities for dialogue on climate change between business and religious leaders and communities. *(p. 138)*

Recommendation #16: Establish religious outreach efforts on climate change tailored specifically to certain regions of the United States and their own religious traditions, especially the U.S. South. *(p. 139)*

Recommendation #17: Continue to develop and expand the field of Religion and Ecology, and its ability to unearth the commonalities across religions on matters of ecology and to supply language, concepts and textual support to religious leaders who want to articulate environmental issues to their constituencies. (See, for example, *www.environment.harvard.edu/religion.*) *(p. 139)*

Recommendation #18: Reach out to seminaries and other religious training institutions and encourage them to incorporate climate change into their curricula for new religious leaders. Provide education on climate change to current clergy via continuing education and other means. *(p. 139)*

Recommendation #19: Establish religion-science and religion-environmentalist partnerships on environmental issues. *(p. 140)*

POLITICS

Recommendation #20: Design and execute a "New Vision for Energy" campaign to encourage a national market-based transition to alternative energy sources. Harness multiple messages tailored to different audiences that embed the climate change issue in a larger set of co-benefit narratives, such as: reducing U.S. dependency on Middle East oil (national security); penetrating global export markets with American innovations (U.S. stature); boosting U.S. job growth (jobs); and cutting local air pollution (health). *(p. 149)*

Recommendation #21: Recast climate change as a moral and faith issue, not a scientific or environmental one. Catalyze a broader coalition of allies around this moral common ground. *(p. 151)*

Recommendation #22: Increase the emphasis on adaptation and preparedness for climate change, both because it is warranted based on climate change we are already committed to, but also because it could be a back door to a more reality-based dialogue about mitigation. *(p. 152)*

Recommendation #23: Recruit a group of party elders from both parties who are less ensconced in the gridlock of today's Washington, D.C., and would be more able to work together to promote constructive action on climate change among the incumbents in their party. *(p. 152)*

Recommendation #24: Convene a group of political scientists, elected officials (and their staffers), and campaign operatives to conduct an analysis and dialogue about the connections between systemic problems in democratic governance in the United States and climate change. For example, how do campaign financing, redistricting and the lack of competitive seats and other factors influence policy performance on climate change? *(p. 153)*

ENTERTAINMENT & ADVERTISING

Recommendation #25: Create a new overarching communications entity or project to design and execute a well-financed public education campaign on climate change science and its implications. This multi-faceted campaign would leverage the latest social science findings concerning attitude formation and change on climate change, and would use all available media in an effort to disseminate rigorously accurate information, and to counter disinformation in real time. *(p. 159)*

Recommendation #26: Undertake systematic and rigorous projects to test the impact of environmental communications in all media (e.g., advertising, documentary, feature film) on civic engagement, public opinion and persuasive outcomes. Use these to inform new creative work on multi-media climate change communications. *(p. 161)*

Recommendation #27: Embed messages about climate change into a variety of existing communications channels, such as weathercasting and entertainment vehicles. *(p. 162)*

EDUCATION

Recommendation #28: Improve K-12 students' understanding of climate change by promoting it as a standards-based content area within science curricula and incorporating it into other disciplinary curricula and teacher certification standards. Use the occasion of the state reviews of science standards for this purpose, which are being prompted by the states' need to comply with the Fall 2007 start of high-stakes science testing under the No Child Left Behind Act. *(p. 169)*

Recommendation #29: Organize a grassroots educational campaign to create local narratives around climate change impacts and solutions, while mobilizing citizen engagement and action. Kick the campaign off with a National Climate Week that would recur on an annual basis. *(p. 171)*

Recommendation #30: Identify and execute opportunities to incorporate climate change content into instructional technologies, devices and software products, including video games and educational simulations such as SimCity™. *(p. 173)*

Recommendation #31: Create a variety of academic and non-academic competitions centered on climate change, or harness existing competitions by introducing climate change as a topic. *(p. 174)*

Recommendation #32: Following the trend toward niche channels and narrowcasting, create a TV show or entire channel dedicated to educational and engaging coverage of all dimensions of climate change, ranging from the natural sciences to policy developments in the United States and abroad. *(p. 174)*

BUSINESS & FINANCE

Recommendation #33: The Business & Finance working group at the Conference composed an eight-principle framework, and proposed that it be disseminated broadly to trade associations and individual business leaders (especially at the CEO and board level) as a set of clear and feasible actions that businesses can and should take on climate change. *(p. 181)*

Recommendation #34: Create and fund an R&D organization to undertake and disseminate credible and independent studies of the economic impacts of climate change on business sectors and specific businesses at a level of detail sufficient to affect decision-making. The organization would complement this data by also offering credible information on available solutions, especially energy efficiency investments with rapid paybacks and high rates of return. *(p. 185)*

Recommendation #35: Launch a certification program and logo signifying climate-friendly products and services, or rationalize such efforts already in existence in order to concentrate consumer awareness and purchasing power on behalf of climate change mitigation objectives. *(p. 186)*

ENVIRONMENTALISTS & CIVIL SOCIETY

Recommendation #36: Create a broad-based Climate Action Leadership Council of 10-12 recognizable and senior eminent leaders from all key national sectors and constituencies to serve as an integrating mechanism for developing and delivering a cohesive message to society about the seriousness of climate change and the imperative of taking action. The Council would include leaders from business, labor, academia, government, the NGO sector, the professions (medicine, law, and public health) and community leaders. They would be chosen on the basis of their credibility within their respective communities, but also across society at large. *(p. 192)*

Recommendation #37: In order to scale up and bring in the required resources, expand the number of donors who understand the urgency of climate change and work with them to identify action-oriented grants consistent with their funding mission and style. *(p. 195)*

Recommendation #38: Create an environmental corps of college students to lead research and action on climate change. This would range from promoting greenhouse gas reduction pledges by their respective colleges and universities to undertaking action beyond their institutions. *(p. 195)*

Recommendation #39: Create one or more competitions among the 200+ U.S. mayors who pledged to voluntarily fulfill the Kyoto Protocol target, whereby their cities would seek to best one another on some specific and measurable climate change-related metric, such as the most compact fluorescent light bulbs installed within a year. *(p. 195)*

Participants

Yale School of Forestry & Environmental Studies Conference on Climate Change
October 6-8, 2005

The Yale F&ES Conference "Climate Change: From Science to Action" brought together 110 eminent leaders and thinkers from across a broad spectrum to consider how to move the U.S. from the science of climate change to more effective action. This document reflects their collective insights, wisdom, and ideas from their two and a half days together. Biographies for this group can be found at http://environment.yale.edu/climate.

Daniel R. Abbasi, Director of the Yale Conference, is an Associate Dean at the Yale School of Forestry & Environmental Studies and directs the Environmental Attitudes and Behavior project at the Yale Center for Environmental Law & Policy.

Edward P. Bass of Fort Worth, Texas, is extensively involved in business, conservation, and ranching and serves on the boards of numerous national and international conservation and ecological concerns.

Frank R. Baumgartner is Distinguished Professor of Political Science at Penn State University. His work focuses on public policy, agenda-setting, and interest groups in American politics.

Frances G. Beinecke is President of the Natural Resources Defense Council.

Susan Bell is Vice President for The William and Flora Hewlett Foundation.

David E. Blockstein is a Senior Scientist with the National Council for Science and the Environment.

Stephen Bocking is Professor of Environmental Politics and History at Trent University in Canada.

Cynthia M. Brill is General Counsel for Verified Identity Pass, Inc.

Steven Brill is the founder and CEO of Verified Identity Pass, The American Lawyer, Court TV, and Brill's Content, among other ventures.

Jeff Burnside is a television news reporter, producer, anchor and news manager for WTVJ NBC 6 Special Projects Unit in Miami, Florida.

Deb Callahan is the immediate past President of the League of Conservation Voters.

Jessica H. Catto is President of Crockett Street Management, LLC and a founder of Elk Mountain Builders, Inc. in Colorado.

Marian R. Chertow is Director of the Industrial Environmental Management Program at the Yale School of Forestry & Environmental Studies.

Benson Chiles is the founder of Blue Line, a strategic consulting network for environmental and public interest organizations.

Reverend Richard Cizik is Vice President for Governmental Affairs of the National Association of Evangelicals.

Eileen Claussen is President of the Pew Center on Global Climate Change and Strategies for the Global Environment.

Kevin J. Coyle is Vice President for Education at the National Wildlife Federation.

Susan Crown is a Principal of Henry Crown and Company and serves as President of the Arie and Ida Crown Memorial, a private foundation established in 1947.

Lisa Curran is Associate Professor of Tropical Resources and Director of the Tropical Resources Institute at the Yale School of Forestry & Environmental Studies.

Steve Curwood is Executive Producer and Host of "Living on Earth" on National Public Radio.

Fred C. Danforth is Managing Partner of Sustainable Land Ventures in Maine and the lead partner for Nevada Spring Creek Partners in Montana's Blackfoot Valley.

Cornelia Dean is a science writer and commentator at The New York Times.

Jim DiPeso is Policy Director of REP America, the national grassroots organization of Republicans for environmental protection.

Strachan Donnelley is founder and President of the Center for Humans and Nature, and serves on several non-profit boards, including the Land Institute and the Gaylord and Dorothy Donnelley Foundation.

Diane Doucette is Director of the Climate California Campaign at Redefining Progress.

Barrett I. Duke, Jr. is Vice President for Public Policy and Research and also Director of the Research Institute of The Ethics & Religious Liberty Commission, the Southern Baptist Convention's agency for applied Christianity.

Robert Edgar is General Secretary of the National Council of the Churches of Christ in the USA.

John R. Ehrmann is a founder and Senior Partner of the Meridian Institute.

David Elisco is the Series Producer of Sea Studios Foundation and served in that capacity for phase one of the television series *Strange Days on Planet Earth.*

William B. Ellis is Senior Visiting Fellow at the Yale School of Forestry & Environmental Studies and former CEO of Northeast Utilities, New England's largest electric and gas utility.

Daniel C. Esty is the Hillhouse Professor of Environmental Law and Policy at Yale University and Director of the Yale Center for Environmental Law and Policy.

David Fenton is the founder & CEO of Fenton Communications.

Jesse Fink is President and CEO of Marshall Street Management.

Baruch Fischhoff is Howard Heinz University Professor in the Department of Social and Decision Sciences and the Department of Engineering and Public Policy at Carnegie Mellon University, where he is head of the Center for Integrated Study of Human Dimensions of Global Change.

Maggie Fox is Deputy Director of the Sierra Club.

Al Franken is an Emmy Award-winning television writer and producer, best-selling author, Grammy-winning comedian, and now host of The Al Franken Show on Air America Radio.

Ellen V. Futter is President of the American Museum of Natural History.

Michel Gelobter is the Executive Director of Redefining Progress.

Bradford S. Gentry is Senior Lecturer and Director of the Research Program on Private Investment and the Environment at the Yale School of Forestry & Environmental Studies.

Peter C. Goldmark, Jr. is Director of the Climate and Air Program at Environmental Defense, after serving as CEO of the International Herald Tribune, President of the Rockefeller Foundation, and Executive Director of the Port Authority of New York and New Jersey.

The Honorable Al Gore is Chairman of Generation Investment Management, Chairman of Current TV, on the Board of Directors of Apple Computer, a Senior Advisor to Google, and a Visiting Professor at Middle Tennessee State University in Murfreesboro, Tennessee.

Paul Gorman is the Executive Director of the National Religious Partnership for the Environment.

Walter E. Grazer is Policy Advisor for Religious Liberty, Human Rights and European Affairs and Director of the Environmental Justice Program for the United States Catholic Conference.

Melanie C. Green is Assistant Professor of Psychology at the University of North Carolina, Chapel Hill.

John Grim is a co-founder and co-Director with Mary Evelyn Tucker of the Forum on Religion and Ecology at Harvard University.

Arnulf M. Grubler is Professor in the field of Energy and Technology at the Yale School of Forestry & Environmental Studies and senior research scholar at the International Institute for Applied Systems Analysis in Laxenburg, Austria.

F. Henry Habicht II is Chief Executive Officer of the Global Environment & Technology Foundation, a founding Principal of Capital E, LLC, and serves as Commissioner on the National Commission on Energy Policy.

James T. Hamilton is the Charles S. Sydnor Professor of Public Policy, Economics, and Political Science at Duke University.

Hal Harvey is the Environment Program Director at the William and Flora Hewlett Foundation.

Susan J. Hassol is a researcher and writer, the author of *Impacts of a Warming Arctic, The Synthesis Report of the Arctic Climate Impact Assessment,* and the screenplay for HBO's film on climate change, "Too Hot Not to Handle."

David G. Hawkins is Director of the Climate Center at the Natural Resources Defense Council.

Teresa Heinz is the chairman of the Howard Heinz Endowment and the Heinz Family Philanthropies.

Harrison Hickman is a founding partner of Global Strategy Group, LLC.

Anthony C. Janetos is Vice President of the H. John Heinz III Center for Science, Economics and the Environment.

M. Albin Jubitz, Jr. is a retired businessman and environmental activist.

Martin S. Kaplan has a general corporate law and trust practice at Wilmer Cutler Pickering Hale and Dorr LLP.

Randall Katz is President and CEO of Milestone Entertainment, developers of innovative, patented game concepts for use in all electronic media from television to mobile phones to the Internet.

Stephen R. Kellert is the Tweedy/Ordway Professor of Social Ecology and Co-Director of the Hixon Center for Urban Ecology at the Yale School of Forestry & Environmental Studies.

The Honorable John F. Kerry represents Massachusetts in the United States Senate.

Carl W. Knobloch, Jr. is president and CEO of West Hill Investors in Atlanta.

Elizabeth Kolbert is a staff writer for *The New Yorker*. Her award winning series "The Climate of Man" is being incorporated into her new book, *Field Notes from a Catastrophe: Man, Nature, and Climate Change*, published in March 2006.

Richard E. Kroon is recently retired as Managing Partner and Chairman of the Sprout Group Venture Capital Fund.

Jon A. Krosnick is Frederic O. Glover Professor in Humanities and Social Sciences in the Department of Political Science at Stanford University and Director of the Stanford Methods of Analysis Program in the Social Sciences.

Steven Kull is Director of the Program on International Policy Attitudes at the University of Maryland and Editor of *World Public Opinion.org*.

William C. Kunkler is Executive Vice President for CC Industries, Inc., a private equity firm focused on manufacturing companies and real estate investments. He is also Vice President of Henry Crown and Company, the parent company of CCI.

George Lakoff is Professor of Linguistics at the University of California, Berkeley.

Gara LaMarche is Vice President and Director of U.S. Programs for the Open Society Institute.

Jonathan Lash is President of the World Resources Institute.

Congressman James A. Leach represents Iowa in the U.S. House of Representatives.

Deborah Levin is President of the Environmental Media Association.

Eugene Linden is an environmental writer. His latest book is *The Winds of Change: Climate, Weather, and the Destruction of Civilizations,* published in 2006.

Amory Lovins is the founder and President of The Rocky Mountain Institute.

Mindy S. Lubber is President of Ceres.

Jane Lubchenco is Wayne and Gladys Valley Professor of Marine Biology and Distinguished Professor of Zoology at Oregon State University.

Arthur Lupia is Professor of Political Science and Research Professor at the Institute for Social Research at the University of Michigan.

Jerry Mahlman, for many years at NOAA's Geophysical Fluid Dynamics Laboratory at Princeton University, currently holds a part-time position at the National Center for Atmospheric Research in Boulder, CO, and as a consultant to the Pew Center on Global Climate Change in Washington, D.C.

Michael B. McElroy is the Gilbert Butler Professor of Environmental Studies at Harvard University.

Ronald Edward Nordhaus is an author, researcher, and political strategist. In the fall of 2006, Houghton Mifflin will publish his book *The Death of Environmentalism and the Birth of a New American Politics,* co-authored with Michael Shellenberger.

Carl Pope is Executive Director of the Sierra Club.

Robert Repetto is a Senior Advisor to Stratus Environmental Consulting, Inc. in Boulder, Colorado, Fellow of the Tim Wirth Chair in the Graduate School of Public Affairs at the University of Colorado, and Professor in the Practice of Sustainable Development at the Yale School of Forestry & Environmental Studies.

John A. Riggs is Executive Director of the Program on Energy, the Environment, and the Economy at The Aspen Institute.

James E. Rogers is Chairman, President and CEO of Cinergy Corp.

Jonathan P. Rose is President of Jonathan Rose Companies, LLC.

Auden Schendler is Director of Environmental Affairs at the Aspen Skiing Company.

Oswald J. Schmitz is Professor of Population and Community Ecology, Associate Dean of Academic Affairs at the School of Forestry & Environmental Studies, and Director of the Center for Biodiversity and Conservation Science at Yale University.

Stephen H. Schneider is at Stanford University, where he has appointments as the Melvin and Joan Lane Professor for Interdisciplinary Environmental Studies in the Department of Biological Sciences, the Center for Environmental Science and Policy, the Department of Civil Engineering and the Center for Environmental Science and Policy.

Mark Schwartz is the immediate past President and Chief Executive Officer of Soros Fund Management.

Larry J. Schweiger is President and CEO of the National Wildlife Federation.

John S. Scurci is Principal of J. Scurci & Co.

Peter A. Seligmann is Chairman of the Board and CEO of Conservation International.

Edward Skloot is Executive Director of the Surdna Foundation.

Theodore M. Smith is Executive Director of the Henry P. Kendall Foundation in Boston, Massachusetts.

Richard C. J. Somerville is Distinguished Professor at Scripps Institution of Oceanography, University of California, San Diego.

Patrick Spears is co-founder and President of the Intertribal Council on Utility Policy, representing ten tribes in the Dakotas and Nebraska.

James Gustave Speth is Dean and Professor in the Practice of Environmental Policy and Sustainable Development at the Yale School of Forestry & Environmental Studies.

Vikki N. Spruill is President of SeaWeb, a non-profit organization that uses strategic communications and social marketing techniques to advance ocean conservation.

Adam C. Stern is the Executive Director of the Coalition on the Environment and Jewish Life.

Todd Stern, former Assistant to President Clinton and Staff Secretary and Counselor to Secretary of the Treasury Lawrence Summers, is a partner at Wilmer Cutler Pickering Hale and Dorr.

Mark Stoler is Director of Environment, Health & Safety Operations for General Electric Company.

Ellen Susman is Producer and Host of *Superwoman Central*, a weekly Houston PBS television program.

Stephen Daily Susman is the founder of the Susman Godfrey law firm, specializing in commercial litigation.

Mitchell Thomashow is Chair of the Antioch New England Department of Environmental Studies. He will become President of Unity College in July 2006.

Mary Evelyn Tucker is Research Associate at the Harvard-Yenching Institute and, with John Grim, co-founder and co-Director of the Harvard Forum on Religion and Ecology.

John P. Wargo is Professor of Environmental Risk Analysis and Policy at the School of Forestry & Environmental Studies, Professor of Political Science, and Director of the Environment and Health Initiative at Yale University.

Ruth H. Whitney is Chief of Staff to the Attorney General of Arkansas.

The Honorable Timothy E. Wirth is the President of the United Nations Foundation and Better World Fund.

Wren W. Wirth is President of the Winslow Foundation.

Richard B. Wirthlin is President and founder of Wirthlin Worldwide and served as Chief Strategist to former U.S. President Ronald Reagan.

Adam R. Wolfensohn is a New York-based producer of environmental documentaries. His current film, entitled *Melting Planet,* is on schedule for theatrical release in 2006.

George M. Woodwell founded the Woods Hole Research Center in Woods Hole, Massachusetts, in 1985 and served as its director until 2005.

About the Author

Daniel R. Abbasi, Director of the 2005 Yale F&ES Conference on Climate Change, is an Associate Dean at the Yale School of Forestry & Environmental Studies and Director of the Environmental Attitudes and Behavior project at the Yale Center for Environmental Law & Policy.

He is also an advisor to MSM Capital Partners, which invests in business platforms and low-carbon technologies to mitigate climate change. Prior to Yale, Mr. Abbasi was an executive in the for-profit education sector with the Kaplan, Inc. unit of the Washington Post Company and a strategy and M&A professional at Time Warner. He served as Senior Adviser in the Office of Policy at the U.S. Environmental Protection Agency from 1993-1996, working on climate change, trade, public/private environmental technology partnerships, sustainable development, regulatory innovation, and public communications.

Mr. Abbasi has experience as an environmental issues specialist on a winning presidential campaign, as an international correspondent for the Earth Times newspaper, and managing a project on corporate accounting for environmental costs and risks at the World Resources Institute. He has also been a dispute resolution specialist for the American Arbitration Association and was Associate Director of the Stanford Center on Conflict and Negotiation at Stanford University. He holds a BA, magna cum laude, from Harvard College, an MBA from Harvard Business School, and an MA in Political Science from Stanford University.

Yale School of Forestry & Environmental Studies

PUBLICATION SERIES

To capture exciting environmental projects at Yale of interest to a broad professional audience, the Yale School of Forestry & Environmental Studies Publication Series issues selected work by Yale faculty, students, and colleagues each year in the form of books, bulletins, working papers and reports. All publications since 1995 are available for order as bound copies, or as free downloadable pdfs, at our online bookstore at *www.yale.edu/environment/publications*. Publications are produced using a print-on-demand system and printed on recycled paper. For further information or inquiries, contact Jane Coppock, Editor of the F&ES Publication Series, at jane.coppock@yale.edu.